CU01498142

OPTIMIZE YOUR TRADING EDGE

OPTIMIZE YOUR TRADING EDGE

Increase Profits, Reduce
Draw Downs, and Eliminate
Leaks in Your Trading Strategy

BO YODER

New York   Chicago   San Francisco   Lisbon   London
Madrid   Mexico City   Milan   New Delhi   San Juan
Seoul   Singapore   Sydney   Toronto

1 2 3 4 5 6 7 8 9 0   DOC/DOC   0 9 8 7

ISBN 978–0–07–149846–3
MHID   0–07–149846–X

This publication is designed to provide accurate and authoritative information in regard to the subject matter covered. It is sold with the understanding that the publisher is not engaged in rendering legal, accounting, or other professional service. If legal advice or other expert assistance is repuired, the services of a competent professional person should be sought.

> —*From a declaration of principles jointly adopted by a committee of the American Bar Association and a committee of publishers.*

McGraw-Hill books are available at special quantity discounts to use as premiums and sales promotions, or for use in corporate training programs. For more information, please write to the Director of Special Sales, Professional Publishing, McGraw-Hill, Two Penn Plaza, New York, NY 10121–2298. Or contact your local bookstore.

Library of Congress Cataloging-in-Publication Data

Yoder, Bo.
   Optimize your trading edge : increase profits, reduce draw-downs, and eliminate leaks in your trading strategy / Bo Yoder.
      p. cm.
ISBN–13: 978–0–07–149846–3 (hbk. : alk. paper)
ISBN–10: 0–07–149846–X
1. Speculation. 2. Investments. I. Title.
HG6015.Y63 2008
332.64'5—dc22   2007035221

For my mother, who always knew she would live to see the day ... no matter what it was I tried to accomplish.

CONTENTS

INTRODUCTION

When I first began trading, I approached the markets from a fundamentally driven "investment" mentality. I looked for "value stocks" and the opportunity to buy into great companies at a discount. I defined these opportunities by analyzing a business from the ground up—a labor intensive process that often failed to yield fruit. The majority of the companies that I analyzed were defined as bloated and overvalued by my analysis structure. Yet it was these "bad" stocks that delivered astounding gains again and again as my "good" stocks languished on the sidelines of the trend. I soon became a disciple of the philosophy that *the way to make money in the market is to find a trend that is based on a false premise and to ride that trend until just before it is disproven.*

I began to realize that the markets, much like politics, are driven by a "perception becomes reality" mindset. It did not matter what the stock's true objective value was; rather, what mattered was the crowd's *perception* of the asset's attractiveness and profit potential! If a stock or sector was faddish and "in," the crowd would bid its price up to astronomic levels before reality was forced upon them by the cold shower of an earnings report. I came to believe that greed and fear, psychology, and order flow are what drove the stocks with the highest profit potential. I began to look at price and volume information as the "fundamentals" that determined investment performance and built a new reactionary trading model that let the market's actions dictate my investment decisions.

As this new investment philosophy began to perform for me, I began to spend more time looking at the mathematics and mechanics of edge. I developed entry tactics that radically increased the profit potential of my favorite trading patterns, and my transformation from fundamentalist to chart reader/edge analyst was complete. Much has been written about trade acquisition, but rarely do we see a full discussion of the mechanics that actually deliver a profitable trading strategy. I hope the ideas presented in this book will help change the way you think about edge and enhance your future interactions in the financial world. They are the result of years of research, thousands of trades, and are the distillation of my years of trading the world's markets. I hope they bring you a new level of freedom and profitability as you optimize your trading edge!

Good luck and good trading!

CHAPTER 1

WHAT IS "EDGE"?

The winner's edge is not in a gifted birth, a high IQ, or in talent. The winner's edge is all in the attitude, not aptitude. Attitude is the criterion for success.

— DENIS WAITLEY

The human is an animal hardwired for aggressive risk-taking. Our ancient ancestors, when not risking personal safety in a dangerous world also invented games of chance. There is evidence that gambling games were played more than 4,000 years ago in the ancient civilizations of China, Egypt, and Rome.

These ancient games of chance were often played with a square bone taken from the ankles of sheep or deer. Eventually, manufactured dice began to appear made out of ivory and stone. A set of ivory dice from approximately 1500 B.C. were found in Egypt, and by 900 B.C. the Etruscans had started to create dice with numbers that would look familiar to any Las Vegas stick man.

In ancient times, these games of chance were very much a part of the superstitious and religious experience of civilizations. Probability theory and mathematics had yet to be developed, and so these ancient gamblers truly believed that the gods themselves controlled the outcome of every roll. These days, just about any person on the planet would understand that the majority of these ancient games of chance were pure gambles, devoid of any statistical probability bias other then the physical imperfections of the dice themselves. Since the rules of the games delivered a simple win or a loss, like flipping a coin, the outcome after a long night of gambling was determined by the mechanics of the game, not the mathematics of the payout structure. Therefore, our examination of edge begins not in ancient Egypt, but in Pavia, Italy in 1560.

Rules of the Gamble

Gerolamo Cardano was a mathematician, physician, astrologer, but most importantly a gambler during the Italian Renaissance. A friend of Leonardo da Vinci, Cardano is perhaps best remembered for his algebraic achievements. In the 1560s,he wrote a book entitled *Liber de Ludo Aleae. (Book on Games of Chance)* but it was only published after his death in 1663. *Games of Chance* is believed to be the first book on systematic treatment of probability as related to games of chance. In this book Cardano lays out the principles of dice probability that we all take for granted today. By answering the question "What are the odds that my next throw will be a 2?" *mathematically,* Cardano was the first to investigate the outcome of a dice roll as something other than the will of the gods.

This shift in thinking seems like a simple thing, yet it had profound effects. Think of it from the perspective of a gambler in the seventeenth century. Once you understand that the gods don't control the outcome of every roll, then you can begin to study and understand the possibility that the game's results can be accurately predicted based on the rules of the gamble. If the rules are biased toward one player, then that person can be said to experience a statistical advantage or "edge" over their opponent.

This brings us to the following definitions and their principles:

A fair game, such as a coin toss for stakes of $1 a throw, offers no statistical advantage to either player. In the short-term, one player may experience a short-term statistical anomaly that delivers a "lucky win streak," but over time, the two gambling coin tossers will end up right back where they started. The odds that one particular player will win the next toss are 50 percent. The odds that the flip will produce a loss are also 50 percent.

An advantage game, however, offers a statistical advantage or edge to one player. This advantage may be overt, (if the die rolls 1, 2, 3, or 4, I win, 5, or 6 you win), or mathematically based (I flip heads, I win $2; if I flip tails, I lose $1).

As an example of this principle, consider the following advantage game. You challenge an opponent to roll one die and correctly predict its outcome. You offer to pay this opponent $4 for every $1 that is bet if they roll the number they predicted.

Even though the large payout of this wager seems attractive on the surface, the rules of this game are strongly biased in your favor. The longer you play the game according to these rules, the larger your expected profit. Since the outcome is being determined by a mechanical probability system, (a six-sided die), the exact advantage or edge can be calculated by thinking through all the possible outcomes of the game in a logical manner.

We know that the die has six sides, and therefore has a one in six chance of matching any particular numerical prediction on the following roll. According to the rules of the game, one of the six sides will be the number your opponent predicted and will result in a $4 loss. The probability that this will occur on any given roll is 16.66 percent (1/6). However, five of the six sides will cause your opponent to lose the bet and will generate a $1 profit. The probability that this will occur on any given roll is 83.33 percent (5/6).

If the game is played but once, there is a 16.66 percent chance that you could lose $4. However, the longer you play, the closer the results will come to the statistical probabilities. At the end of 100 rolls, you would expect to have won the $1 wager 83 times for a total profit of $83. Your opponent can be expected to have won $4 from you 17 times out of the hundred rolls, delivering a loss of $68. Subtract these losses from your gains and you would have a net profit of $15. This $15 profit is the result of your edge in this particular wager. Expressed as a percentage, this particular game should deliver a 15 percent profit on every dollar wagered in profits to the advantaged player.

If your opponent regularly wagers $1, then your statistically expressed profit expectation would be 15 cents every time a die is rolled. If a new opponent hears about your game and wishes to participate by wagering $100 on every roll, then your statistical profit expectation would be $15 every time the die is rolled! Seeing the potential this edge offers you, you invite 10 players to your house the following evening. Everyone arrives as planned, and begins the evening wagering $20 on every roll. This means $200 are wagered each time the die is cast. With a 15 percent advantage, this level of wagering will put $30 per roll in your pocket over time. If the die is rolled 100 times per hour, then your game should generate revenue of approximately $3,000 per hour!

Power of a Statistical Edge

The power of this type of statistical edge is the reason why casino operators in Las Vegas can afford to spend a billion dollars building a magnificent casino in an attempt to attract players to come play their house advantaged games. To better understand the power that a statistical advantage delivers to the casino operator, let's analyze the edge a casino enjoys at the roulette table.

A U.S. roulette wheel has 38 numbered slots. Each player places wagers on the felt in an attempt to guess the outcome of the next spin. The players may bet on individual numbers (one through thirty-six), combinations of numbers, or simply red or black (18 of the numbers are black, 18 are red). Although the rules and payouts can seem complicated, the reason that the casino enjoys a strong edge at the roulette table is a simple one … Two of the slots are numbered zero! If the ball happens to land in either of these locations, all the standard bets are lost, and the "house" banks a large profit.

The simplest of bets would be a wager that on the next spin the ball will land on a red or black number. If you bet $10 on red, there are 18 red numbers that would produce a win of $10, and 18 black numbers plus the two zeros that would produce a loss of $10. If we apply Cardano's probability studies to this wager, we realize that if we exclude the zeros, this would be a fair wager. Without the zeros, we would expect to see the ball drop into the slot with the correct color 50 times out of 100. But there is a 5.26 percent chance (2 slots out of 38) on each spin the ball will fall in one of the zero slots, and this skews the probabilities in favor of the casino. With a 5.26 percent advantage, the casino expects to realize profits of $5.26 for every $100 wagered. With an average of 45 spins per hour at a Las Vegas casino, you can see how quickly the profits add up.

The edges that the casino enjoys on the most common games of chance are often quite rich. These statistical advantages are mechanically based, and therefore can be estimated and predicted with extreme accuracy *if the sample size is large enough*. This is why you will see so many tables within the typical casino layout. With only one roulette table, the casino would suffer the ups and downs that the natural variance of their edge delivers. If the casino operator has 10 roulette tables, or even better 100 roulette tables active across several properties, then the law of large numbers virtually ensures the casino operators their 5.26 percent advantage.

As a frame of reference, here are the edges that the house enjoys for the standard casino games.

Craps (Pass line)	1.41%
Roulette	5.26%
Slot Machines	8–15%
Baccarat	1.29%
Casino War (Surrender)	3.73%
Blackjack	5.9% (Near 1% if strategy is used)

Fundamentals of Probability

The law of large numbers is one of the fundamental theories of probability. It states that as the sample size or number of independent repetitions grows, the closer the average of the past outcomes approaches the statistical prediction of the probable outcome. Simply put, the larger the sample size, the greater the odds that the results of any random event will match its statistical probability of occurrence. This theory was first described by the Swiss mathematician Jacob Bernoulli at the end of the fifteenth century. His book *Ars Conjectandi (The Art of Conjecturing)*, published posthumously in 1713, is thought to be one of the founding documents of mathematic probability.

To prove the law of large numbers, or Bernoulli's theorem, look at the probabilities of a dice roll. Since there are six sides on a die, it can be stated that there is a 1 in 6 chance that the number five will be rolled on any given trial. While this statistical probability is absolute, the chance that five will be seen once every six times the die rolled is not that great. Only when the sample size is large enough can we have a high degree of confidence that the number of fives rolled will be one in six.

A series of trials will allow you to experience, visually, how the law of large numbers works. Get yourself three pair of dice. Roll the six dice 100 times and note how many times the number five appears. Statistically speaking, the number five should appear once in each roll. The number five should appear 10 times in ten rolls and a total of 60 times over the course of the 100 roll experiment. Believing in the law of large numbers, I have no confidence that the first roll will produce a five, moderate confidence that the number five will be seen approximately ten times in the first ten rolls, and extreme confidence that the number five will be seen 60 times by the time the experiment has ended

2	6	6	6	4	2	Fives = 0

Not one five is seen in the first roll!

3	3	1	2	5	6	Fives = 1
2	2	6	1	5	5	Fives = 3
2	2	2	1	6	6	Fives = 3
4	2	2	2	4	6	Fives = 3
5	3	6	5	5	2	Fives = 6
5	4	4	5	5	3	Fives = 9
5	4	2	4	4	5	Fives = 11
6	4	2	3	5	3	Fives = 12
4	6	3	4	6	1	Fives = 12

So after ten rolls, the number five has been seen 12 times. This is two times more then the statistical prediction, and therefore the experiment can be said to be running "hot."

3	5	3	2	3	6	Fives	=	13
6	4	6	5	4	1	Fives	=	14
2	4	5	3	5	3	Fives	=	15

On the last three rolls, the number 5 was seen once each roll. This outcome is "statistically perfect," but due to natural statistical variance will be quite rare.

6	4	6	2	3	2	Fives	=	15
4	1	5	6	2	1	Fives	=	16
3	6	1	1	4	4	Fives	=	16
2	6	5	2	6	3	Fives	=	17
3	6	5	3	3	2	Fives	=	18
3	2	6	2	3	5	Fives	=	19
2	4	1	3	6	2	Fives	=	19

At the end of the 20th roll, only 19 five's have been seen, and the experiment can be said to be running "lean."

4	5	5	6	5	6	Fives	=	22
2	1	5	4	2	1	Fives	=	23
6	5	1	1	1	4	Fives	=	24
2	6	1	3	5	5	Fives	=	26
1	3	3	6	1	6	Fives	=	26
4	1	6	1	5	3	Fives	=	27
5	6	6	1	4	2	Fives	=	28
5	4	4	1	4	1	Fives	=	29
6	6	1	6	5	3	Fives	=	30
5	6	5	3	5	4	Fives	=	33

At the end of 30 rolls, the experiment is again running a bit hot. Instead of the statistically predicted 30, 33 number five's have been seen.

6	5	6	3	2	4	Fives	=	34
2	5	2	5	4	3	Fives	=	36

1	2	6	4	4	2	Fives = 36
1	3	5	1	6	5	Fives = 38
4	3	2	1	2	5	Fives = 39
5	3	4	2	1	2	Fives = 40
1	4	3	6	6	3	Fives = 40
5	1	6	6	2	3	Fives = 41
6	2	3	4	4	3	Fives = 41
4	3	2	3	3	2	Fives = 41
3	1	3	4	5	4	Fives = 42
3	5	5	4	3	3	Fives = 44
1	1	4	4	3	6	Fives = 44
4	2	5	5	6	6	Fives = 46
3	2	3	1	4	6	Fives = 46
1	4	2	4	2	6	Fives = 46
5	3	2	1	4	3	Fives = 47
2	5	1	4	3	2	Fives = 48
1	1	1	3	5	4	Fives = 49
5	2	3	6	1	3	Fives = 50

After 50 rolls, you can see how the law of large numbers is beginning to kick in. With a statistical expectation of 50 five's for 50 rolls, we have seen exactly 50.

6	3	4	5	6	3	Fives = 51
3	4	3	5	1	2	Fives = 52
6	2	4	4	5	1	Fives = 53
3	4	3	1	4	1	Fives = 53
3	3	2	3	5	3	Fives = 54
1	3	3	6	4	6	Fives = 54
2	2	2	3	6	5	Fives = 55
2	5	1	5	1	4	Fives = 57
2	4	2	5	5	2	Fives = 59
4	2	6	5	3	2	Fives = 60
4	1	3	5	5	4	Fives = 62

3	3	4	1	5	3	Fives	=	63
4	3	4	6	4	6	Fives	=	63
4	2	4	3	1	2	Fives	=	63
6	3	4	4	3	2	Fives	=	63
3	2	6	3	6	4	Fives	=	63
5	3	6	6	1	3	Fives	=	64
4	5	2	3	2	2	Fives	=	65
4	2	6	6	2	4	Fives	=	65
6	3	6	5	3	4	Fives	=	66
5	6	5	4	6	4	Fives	=	68
2	1	5	2	2	4	Fives	=	69
4	5	4	6	2	1	Fives	=	70
6	6	6	2	1	2	Fives	=	70
5	4	6	4	4	5	Fives	=	72
1	3	3	6	6	5	Fives	=	73
6	5	3	5	3	5	Fives	=	76
2	3	6	4	2	6	Fives	=	76
2	5	4	1	3	1	Fives	=	77
1	5	1	1	6	2	Fives	=	78
5	6	6	4	2	5	Fives	=	79
3	3	4	5	2	4	Fives	=	80
5	5	1	6	5	1	Fives	=	83
6	6	5	5	5	6	Fives	=	86
1	5	6	4	1	5	Fives	=	88
2	5	3	3	2	3	Fives	=	89
4	3	4	1	6	5	Fives	=	90
3	6	2	3	6	3	Fives	=	90
1	4	1	2	1	5	Fives	=	91
5	5	1	6	6	1	Fives	=	93
1	5	2	4	5	1	Fives	=	95
4	2	1	4	1	4	Fives	=	95
1	6	3	2	6	6	Fives	=	95
5	3	2	2	1	1	Fives	=	96
5	6	3	3	1	3	Fives	=	97

1	6	2	5	4	4	Fives = 98
6	4	6	2	4	2	Fives = 98
2	4	1	4	6	2	Fives = 98
5	1	3	5	4	3	Fives = 100
2	4	3	3	3	1	Fives = 100

At the end of the trial, even though at times the numbers ran hot or cold, the law of large numbers delivered the statistically expected result: 100 five's for 100 rolls.

Optimize Your Statistical Advantage

Using casino games to illustrate the edge concept works well, since these games of chance are mechanical in nature. A six-sided die *is what it is*. It has a certain number of sides, and has been constructed the same way for 4000 years. This makes edge analysis a simple exercise in mathematics.

However, the goal of this book is to help you to optimize your advantage in the *financial marketplaces* of the world. These organic entities are constantly changing and shifting in response to emotions, economic pressures, and changes in culture/society. Change is the only constant, and rules can be hard to identify at times. If the casino's edge is at one end of the spectrum of clarity, the financial marketplaces occupy the other extreme. As a way to help you bridge your understanding between the two, let us examine a statistical advantage based business that exists between the extremes.

Sampling and Modeling

If you take a moment to think about it, an insurance policy is at its root a simple wager. You do not believe that you will be involved in an auto accident anytime in the next three months, but the damage such an accident could cause to your finances/health could be extreme. This risk is one you do not wish to assume, so you engage an insurance company in a structured financial wager. You bet them a sum of money that you *will be involved* in an auto accident, and they "fade" your wager. In order to properly price your policy, the insurance company utilizes statistical sampling and modeling to predict with great accuracy your relative odds for catastrophe. They can do so not because they know anything about your driving skills or habits, but because if they insure enough drivers, the law of large numbers will insure that their results closely match their statistical models. A certain number of drivers in your demographic will be involved in accidents, and the size of their claims will average out to a sum near the predicted mean. These losses will be offset by the premiums paid by the rest of the client base, and the difference between the two will be the insurance companies profit for the quarter.

As we have shown in the examples earlier, *edge* or *statistical advantage* is a function of the probability of a losing event versus its positive risk-to-reward ratio. A fair game such as a coin toss or a bet on red at the roulette table can be turned into an edge-filled situation by changing the probabilities (adding two losing slots to a roulette wheel) or adjusting the payout. If I offer you the chance to wager $100 on a coin flip, you might accept this fair game if you feel like an entertaining gamble. But if someone offers you 2 to 1 on your money for the same coin flip, you would run to an ATM to withdraw the max as the statistical advantage you would enjoy with that payout is staggering.

This formula is precisely what the insurance company is analyzing when they write your policy. They look at your driving record, and the driving records of those in your peer groups in an attempt to predict the probability that you would be involved in an accident. Once they have defined this probability, they are in a position to determine what level their risk-to-reward ratio needs to be to ensure them a profit in the long term. The insurance industry deals with miniscule probabilities, therefore they can profitably exist with a large inverse risk-to-reward ratio on their policies. They know that they will be forced to make some big payments as clients get into accidents, but if their initial risk analysis was correct, the thousands of small premiums they collect every month will more than cover these losses.

Profit Expectations

Anytime you make an investment or take a trade within the world's financial markets, you are essentially insuring another trader against loss. When you buy a stock in an up trend on the premise that the trend will continue, the trader who sells you his shares is of a contrary opinion and is abdicating their right to future profits in return for elimination of risk. You assume the risk of loss on the shares you buy in return for the right to capture any profits that may accrue. This difference of opinion (one trader assuming what they feel to be a "good" risk while the other offloads what they feel to be "bad" risk), is the fundamental source of profits in any financial marketplace. Make no mistake about it; trading is a zero sum game. In order for you to realize a profit, another trader must make a poor decision and sell you their risk at a position of disadvantage. Their lost opportunity or outright loss of capital becomes your gain.

Lessons from Poker

Because financial speculation lacks any specific structure or rules set, each trader must decide how they choose to structure their approach toward trend analysis. One of the only gambling games that exhibits this same freedom of choice is poker, and there are many trading lessons to be learned from this popular card game. While there is a rigid structure surrounding hand rankings, betting rounds, and card dealing, outside of that, the game of poker holds an enormous amount of flexibility for individual style. A poker player chooses which hands to play and may change his opening hand requirements based on his analysis of an opponents' playing style or the current betting situation. A hand can be stolen on a bluff without ever having to prove the value of a hand. Some hands have immediate starting value, while others are worthless at the moment, but have the potential to win large sums of money if the correct card falls during the deal.

Poker can act as an accurate proxy for the financial markets, and is a useful tool to use in order to better understand these concepts. I have long used poker analogies and examples to help my consulting clients understand the concepts of the edge as we work to optimize the profitability of their trading strategies. Because a poker game is heavily influenced by the personality/psychology of its participants, this analysis process is a great deal more complex than simple roulette examples. Because of this added "humanity," there can be a surprising difference between mathematically derived edge and the real world experience! A mathematically perfect strategy assumes that your opponents will *always* play in a predictable manner, and as any poker player knows this is an extremely rare occurrence. For the sake of simplicity, assume that each of these poker situations occurs at a six-person, no limit hold-em table in a friend's basement. When poker is played online or in a major casino, the house takes its edge directly in the form of a "rake," (money taken directly out of each pot as the house fee for play). By assuming these examples occur at an informal "home game," the negative effects of the rake can be ignored.

Due to its television popularity, Texas Hold-em Poker has become the most popular poker variant in the modern casino. Each player is dealt two hidden cards, and then after a series of betting rounds, five community cards are dealt face up on the table. Each player makes the best poker hand possible from these available cards and if a showdown occurs the best hand wins the pot. There is a round of betting after the hidden cards are dealt, then the first three community cards or "the flop" are dealt face up in the middle of the table. At this point most players know whether they have a hand or not, and most will fold during the betting round before the next face up card or "the turn" is dealt. Another round of betting occurs, then the last face up card or "the river" is dealt. Now that the last card has been dealt, there is no room for improvement and the final round of betting occurs.

Let's begin by analyzing the theoretical edge surrounding a mathematically perfect poker strategy. The average winning percentage against one opponent is approximately 81 percent if dealt AA, KK, QQ, or JJ. Against two opponents, the winning percentage drops to 67 percent, so our strategy must include tactics that will help to produce a heads up situation. Our mathematically perfect strategy would be to only play these four hands and to wager all our money in an attempt to drive out all but one opponent. As we know from previous examples, the first step in analyzing edge is to define the probability for success. Since we are only interested in playing AA, KK, QQ, or JJ, there are only 16 cards of interest to us in the deck. The odds that our first hole card will be an A, K, Q, or J is 16/52 or 30 percent. If we are lucky enough to be dealt one of these cards, then we have a 3/51 or nearly 6 percent chance of receiving a card needed to make a pair. Taken concurrently, there is only a 1.8 percent chance (30 percent x 6 percent) that we will be dealt a hand that fits this strategy.

If 50 hands per hour are dealt on average, then you would expect to see two or three playable hands over the course of a three-hour poker evening. If the forced bets or "blinds" are $.50-$1.00, then you would expect to lose $37.50 over the course of the evening in blinds alone. (This "overhead" is quite similar to the transaction costs one incurs when trading a financial market.) If you buy into the game with $100, then it is logical to assume that your bankroll would be approximately $80–$90 by the time a qualifying hand has been dealt. We now have all the parameters needed to simulate this strategy and define its pure mathematical edge.

If you play poker once a week for three hours, then over the course of a year you expect to be dealt a qualifying hand 141 times. You would expect to win 114 times and lose 27. If each pot won or lost averages $90, then your profit for the year would be as follows:

$$141 \text{ wins} \times \$90 = \$12,690$$
$$26 \text{ losses} \times \$90 = \$2,340$$

Gross profits of $10,350 − $1,950 in blinds = net profits of $8,400

$8,400 divided by 141 hands is your profit expectation of approximately $60 per hand. Of course there will be periods when you experience winning or losing streaks, but by the end of the year your sample size will be large enough that your results will smooth themselves out. Or will they? Although this poker strategy is strongly profitable *on paper*, I would be willing to guarantee you that in the real world you lose money playing this way.

The Reality Gap

Because humans are involved, judgment, emotion, and intuition will skew your results. The friends you consistently play poker with will quickly realize that you are only playing the top four pocket pairs. When they see you bet, unless they have one of these hands themselves they will fold. This means that you will rarely win a large pot with your premium hands.

What is worse, when you do get action, it will only be because your opponent has an extraordinarily valuable hand. This tendency will damage your average winning percentage, and as a result the entire strategy model we just analyzed goes out the window. I call the difference between theoretical mathematical edge and experienced edge "the reality gap."

This reality gap is the reason why so many systematic trading models look dreamy in the lab, yet produce nothing but losses and frustrations when taken live into the world's financial markets. In addition to the mathematical potential of any trading strategy, you must analyze the potential for market change. Will this strategy affect the market being traded? How will the strategy's performance change as the market environment shifts? Can you identify which market environment would provide the strongest edge? It is this last question that I believe to be the most important.

CHAPTER 2

THE PAYOUT/PAYBACK CYCLE

... By law of periodical repetition, everything which has happened once must happen again and again—and not capriciously, but at regular periods, and each thing in its own period, not another's and each obeying its own law.

—Mark Twain

I have been working as an edge consultant with individual traders and groups for a number of years. This experience has proven to me again and again one simple fact:

No matter what your trading strategy might be, no matter what time frame, what financial instrument, or analysis structure, the market will endlessly cycle in and out of alignment with your strategy.

Different trading concepts exhibit different levels of cyclicality, but the *payout/payback cycle* is universal to the financially speculative experience.

For every style of trading there will be a "perfect" market environment. When the market is aligned to the strategy that you are trading, every trade will work itself out smoothly, losses will be far and few between, and you will feel on top of the world as your watch your profits accumulate! The excitement and confidence that comes with this *easy money* will grow as your win cluster expands. Unfortunately, these wonderful winning streaks seldom last as long as you might like. Sooner or later the market environment will shift, if ever so slightly, and losses will once again begin to appear. Your accuracy rate will slowly erode and frustration and pain will replace your excitement and elation as the manic-depressive cycle that is trading comes down off its previous high. This constant cycle from "zero" to "hero" and back to "zero" is why I believe speculation as a business has such a high failure rate. The constant and natural shift from market alignment and profits to market misalignment and losses is what I call the *payout/payback cycle*, and it can wreak havoc on your emotions.

I have wasted years of my life in the lab trying to find a way to beat the payback cycle. I believed that if I had a number of valid edges to choose from, I would be able to shift my strategies fast enough to stay with the payout cycle for each trading style as the market environment shifted. This attempt failed completely again and again no matter how inventive or creative my payback cycle avoidance tactics became. I found that instead of staying *ahead* of the payback cycles, I ended up chasing the end of each strategy's individual payout cycle. By the time I had enough data to identify the one particular strategy that was out-performing, the payout cycle in that strategy had just about run its course and was about to cycle back into payback (losses).

Once I came to this realization, I stepped back from this impossible quest and began to specialize. I focused on the trading concepts that had performed well over time and had exhibited a robust edge in every type of market environment. I started to analyze my trading programs from a cyclical perspective and began searching my portfolio of edges to find the concepts that stayed in the payout phase most often. Then I tried to identify which of those strategies offered the most accurate payout/payback cycle predictability.

Profit/Loss Cyclicality

Once I became aware of the profit/loss cyclicality inherent to the payout/payback cycle, my edge analysis processes began to change. I began to see the money flow in and out of these patterns like the tide in the ocean of financial markets. Living near oceans much of my life, I fully understood the power of the ocean's tide. One would certainly never try to stem the tide of the ocean, so what was I doing trying to fight this money tide? I discarded my previous attempts to shift strategies and began to look for ways to work *with the tide* instead of against it. With this changed perspective, I found that I could identify when the market was not aligned to a particular trading style with relative ease. By reducing my trade frequency and aggressiveness during this time of payback, I could avoid taking a number of losses as the strategy first triggered entry signals, and then failed over and over as its market misalignment took its toll.

I had always been aware of the power of loss avoidance as it relates to overall trading edge. However, in the past I had always analyzed loss avoidance in terms of error elimination. If a client came to me averaging two errors per month, then the quickest way to help him increase his profitability was to design a structure to eliminate the errors. Every dollar of loss avoided went directly to the bottom line at month's end. I quickly realized that if I could discover a way to avoid trading losses by applying payout/payback analysis, I could impact my own bottom line with maximum quickness and efficiency.

If I could correctly identify that a particular trading program was in the throes of a payback cycle, then I could pause that strategy until the market climate turned back towards payout. If I could avoid one or two failed setups per cycle, my yearly performance would nearly double. As you might expect, this breakthrough was very exciting to me, and I began to experiment quite successfully with this new concept. As my experience with this new theory grew, my belief in the universal truth of payout/payback cyclicality became more and more profound.

I began to realize that the payout/payback cycle was fundamentally responsible for many of the common errors of emotion and discipline that hurt so many of the traders I worked with in my consulting practice. I saw them get caught up in the euphoria of the payout cycle and begin to get aggressive just as the odds for success begin to shift against them. They would also become discouraged with their trading during a payback cycle and thus abandon otherwise profitable trading strategies in a vain attempt to avoid the pain of loss.

Following is a classic example of payout/payback cycle mismanagement. The example should help you better understand the reality of the damage the payout/payback cycle can cause. Of the several hundred traders/clients I have worked with in recent years, I can count on one hand those who *did not exhibit* some aspect of payout/payback cycle mismanagement. (Since my sample size is large, the law of large numbers lets me state with a high degree of confidence that payout/payback mismanagement is a near universal problem among the trading community.)

Example of Payout/Payback Mismanagement
Trader History

Jack is a trader with a $25,000 trading account.

- He has just discovered a new strategy he plans to begin trading in the S&P 500 Index futures.
- He will risk 1 percent of his account on each trade, and size his positions accordingly.
- He has been trading for a while, but is still rather inexperienced.
- He is *totally unaware* of the existence of the payout/payback cycle.

Jill is a trader with a $25,000 trading account.

- Coincidentally, she has been trading the same strategy that Jack has just discovered.
- She also sizes her positions so as to risk 1 percent of her account on each trade.
- She has been trading for a number of years, and is very experienced.
- She *fully understands* the concept of the payout/payback cycle.

Traders' Interactions with the Markets

As we begin to observe these two traders, they are both enjoying the profitability of the payout cycle. Jill has correctly identified this as a payout market and is more aggressive with her entries. As our test begins, Jack couldn't be happier! After spending several months in the lab working on this new strategy, the first couple of trades have produced a gain! His new edge has begun to prove itself, and he feels certain that now he is going to begin making "big money."

By the end of the first week, the payout cycle is in full effect. Out of the seven trades the strategy gave that week, only one resulted in a loss. Jack's account shows a $1,500 gain for the week, while Jill's aggressive entries into these same setups have delivered a gain of $1,650. As they begin trading the next week, Jill is aware that six wins out of seven possible trades is unusually high. After such a solid week of payout, she knows that the market is likely to begin shifting back toward a payback environment.

Meanwhile, Jack has succumbed to the euphoria of the payout cycle. He decides to increase his position size next week in order to make more money now that he feels his new strategy has been "proven." The first trade Jack takes the following Monday turns out to be a loser. Tuesday's session delivers a small gain, but the easy profitability of the prior week has vanished. Jill has entered the week trading with a cautious posture and notes with emotional objectivity that the setups are beginning to struggle. She decides to trade any valid signals during the next session with half her normal position size.

Jack knows every setup will lose now and again, and remembering the emotionally euphoric high of last week's profitability, justifies the weakness of the last two days as "nothing to be worried about." On Wednesday, the strategy fails badly, and none of the setups that form deliver a profit. Jill interprets this weakness as confirmation that the market has moved from payout to payback. She knows from her historical experience that it will normally take several days for the payback environment to work its way through a full cycle. Therefore, she can predict that the rest of the week is likely to be unprofitable for this trading strategy. She decides to avoid trading in a low or negative expectation environment, and makes plans to take the rest of the week off.

Jack's feelings are hurt by the action of the past few days. He experiences intellectual pain as he observes "his" new strategy failing. In addition, due to his increased position size, the losses sustained this week "hurt" his trading account a great deal more than they would had he stayed with his standard position size. He is unwilling to reduce his position size, because he wants so badly to "make up" his recent losses. He even ponders the possibility of becoming more aggressive in tomorrow's session, responding to the hope that one or two winners with an increased position size will bring him back to the break even point.

Luckily, he overcomes this temptation and decides to trade the same position size in tomorrow's session. As the trading week winds to a close, Jill has enjoyed several days away from her computers. The time away has refreshed her mind and recharged her soul. Jack, on the other hand, has spent his days hunched over his trading screens cursing his "bad luck" as he takes loser after loser. What could possibly have happened? Did he commit some error of trade analysis? Has the edge that worked so wonderfully the week before suddenly vanished? His account shows a $1,700 loss for the week. This is especially frustrating, as not only has he lost all of the profits from the first winning week, but now his account is actually showing red ink! He decides to stop trading and go back into the lab to revisit his research and reassess this trading strategy. Jack spends an intense weekend poring over the charts as he vainly attempts to find a way to beat the payback cycle.

While Jack spends an emotionally exhausting weekend trying to figure out what he did wrong, Jill begins her weekend research refreshed and rejuvenated after her time off. On Sunday she looks at the action she missed, and projects that she would have lost at least $750 on Thursday and Friday. She still lost approximately $500 last week, but feels happy that her identification of the payback cycle and subsequent withdrawal from the markets saved her from taking additional losses. She suspects that after such a terrible string of losing trades, the market is about to shift back to a new payout cycle. Jill looks forward to trading on Monday and in anticipation of payout plans to begin trading with her normal position size.

On Monday the opening bell rings, and Jill begins trading, but the payback cycle is not quite finished. The first trade of the week fails badly and is quickly closed out at a loss. Jack begins trading on Monday in a state of emotional exhaustion. Jack is dead tired from a weekend of intense study in front of his computer and misses entry on the first trade due to a simple lack of focus. He feels rather pleased as he watches the trade fail and the failure leads him to decide to spend the rest of the week paper trading his strategy.

The loss on Monday doesn't cause Jill too much discomfort. She feels confident that the payback cycle is nearing its end. She knows that if this prediction is correct, then another sustained winning streak is just over the horizon. She plans to continue trading normally in tomorrow's session. The next day there are two setups, and they end up producing a small profit. Then on Wednesday, the market builds up a head of steam and begins to trend in earnest. The payout cycle heats up and produces win after win right up until the closing bell on Thursday. Friday's session is a bit more mixed, but still produces a small profit to end the week on a high note.

During this time, Jack has spent the week watching and paper trading his strategy. He feels a bit frustrated that he missed out on the gains from Wednesday and Thursday's session, but is very much relieved to see the strategy producing profits once again. On Friday morning he decides to begin trading again with half-size, "just to get my feet wet." This choice is influenced in large part by the pain he experienced as he missed the last two profitable trades. He feels an urgent need to make up for the profitable trades he missed, and so impulsively jumps back into trading on Friday.

After two solid days of trending action, the market is tired, and the first valid setup on Friday is a loser. Jack feels like he's been had. With hindsight, he can see that his decision to trade this morning was an emotionally based one. Even though his loss for this week was only taken at half size, the mental damage is done.

He quits for the day and then watches in horror as the next setup produces a solid profit. He realizes he missed out on every single profitable trade and that the only trade he actually backed with real money slapped his wrist. He ends the week angry and frustrated, looking back at his second losing week in a row as he heads into the weekend. Jack spends the weekend trying to run away from his feelings. He feels lousy about how his trading is going, and this colors his ability to enjoy the weekend. He drinks too much, eats poorly, and generally spends the weekend in an antisocial sulk.

Jill has had a week of mixed results, but feels happy with how she executed her payout/payback management decisions. While this week was nothing to write home about, it did produce a $750 gain. When the opening bell rings the following Monday, Jill is ready to trade. She makes money during the morning session and heads out for lunch happily looking forward to the rest of the trading week. Jack's funk continues to grow as he misses another winning trade due to sleeping late with a hangover from his overindulgence the night before. "I SHOULD have had that trade!" he mutters to himself, and his feelings of frustration and embarrassment begin to turn to anger.

Tuesday's trade is also a winner, but Jack is now so emotionally distraught that he couldn't bring himself to pull the trigger. His frustration at a peak, he explodes into a full on temper tantrum. "Forget it!" he says as he beats on his keyboard with a fist, "I'm going to trade tomorrow no matter what!" Jack goes to bed early, and gets up the next morning committed and ready to trade. His first trade of the day is a success and is quickly closed out for a nice profit. "I knew it!" he exclaims with a surge of self-righteous indignation. Jack's emotions have been on an incredible emotional roller coaster ride the past few sessions. He has experienced the extreme highs and lows of the "hero to zero" cycle and bears the scars of the anger, frustration, embarrassment, and wish for revenge and retribution that the humiliating "zero" aspect of this cycle creates.

While this up and down ride has been wreaking havoc on Jack's emotional well-being, Jill has been nonchalantly plugging along, trading her plan as she has for several years. Her identification that the market is trading within the context of a payout cycle has allowed her to become more aggressive once again. She increases her position size slightly and squeezes a bit more profit than normal out of every winner. By the middle of the week she is up $1,750 and has yet to experience a loss. Just as before, she knows from experience that when the Midas touch appears, it often brings with it the end of a payout cycle. She begins to trade more cautiously going into Thursday's session. On Thursday and Friday the markets are mixed, and Jill's trading strategy only produces a small gain. Jill is happy to have banked a $2,000 gain for the week, and due to her payout/payback cycle analysis plans to trade cautiously the following Monday.

Jack has had a profitable week and has pulled his account out of its draw down. His gains for the week have put him up nearly $650 for the month. Although he has returned to profitability, Jack is emotionally haggard. He has an air of defeat about him, and plans to trade every pattern next week do or die, and damn the consequences! His rigid mindset is a way to avoid responsibility. By abandoning his trade management and simply trusting to fate, Jack takes no control over his trading or his payout/payback cycle. (A resigned "whatever will be, will be" mind set should be a real danger signal to any trader.)

The Final Week of Our Test

A series of shocking economic announcements buffet the market, and only 2 trades the entire week produce a profit. Jill was expecting a payback cycle, but is surprised at the violence of the chaotic action. She gets caught in one bad position that delivers a greater than expected loss due to slippage, but because she was expecting trouble is able to trade defensively and manages to end the week down just $1,100. By trading conservatively and passing on setups once she identified the payback cycle was in effect, she avoids a $500 loss through the course of the week.

During this chaotic week, Jack has his head down as he trusts the "trading gods" to deliver his profits for him. The last few weeks he has experienced an emotionally painful loss each time he tries to think, so now he just "trades with discipline" and rigidly takes every signal which produces stop after stop after stop. The week has been a particularly bad one for his strategy, and when he quits in disgust at the end of trading on Friday he has lost a total of $1,500. Angry and frustrated, Jack calls his broker and closes out his account. Thus, another trader washes out of the business.

The tragedy is that Jack washed out NOT because his trading strategy lacked the edge, but because he badly mismanaged the payout/payback cycle! He managed to blunder into every mental trap the market can set for a trader, and his behavior turned an edge-filled strategy into a frustration-laden death spiral of fear and anger.

Takeaways

- Jack sat out during a profitable payout cycle, as he waited for confirmation that his setup was working again.
- After observing a win streak, he began trading just as the payout cycle ended and a new payback cycle began.
- Jack lost $1,500 of his trading capital due to his cycle mismanagement.
- Trading the same strategy and utilizing proper cycle management during this period, Jill put more than $2,800 in profits into her bank account!

A solid working knowledge and clear understanding of payout/payback cycle analysis and its management is critical to maintaining a consistent level of performance. Over the course of an average month, proper payout/payback cycle management will result in a much greater return when compared to a trader who is rigidly managing every trade in a systematic manner. The downside to this "feathering" of aggressiveness and position size is that two to three times per year you are likely to encounter an extraordinary payback "super cycle." During these painful and frustrating market environments, price action will be chaotic and unpredictable. The keys used to identify the transition periods from payout to pay back will stop working. Your edge can experience a total breakdown and your win percentage will go into the toilet. (These common chaos super cycles are often what bring edge consulting clients to me after a year killing draw down sweeps through their account.)

It is during one of these chaos periods that you will often begin to hear about market disasters that have produced historic losses for other market participants: hedge funds blowing up, individuals losing a significant portion of their accounts when a stock gaps against them, and devastating limit moves in the futures markets are hallmarks of a payback super cycle.

Learn to Predict Your Payout/Payback Cycle

How does one identify and then learn to predict the payout/payback cycle for your own particular trading strategy? This is one of the key services I provide clients in my consulting practice, as it can result in some remarkable and immediate increases in profitability. I start the process by analyzing a

Insider's Advice   Avoiding larger than usual draw downs is a powerful benefit of edge and payout/payback analysis. Once you become competent at identifying which part of the cycle you are currently experiencing, you will know, based on your historical performance, if the current draw down level is normal or something more serious. When your losses begin to enter this danger zone, the "circuit breakers" in your trading plan will get you out of the market until the trading climate improves.

client's last 20–50 trades. I begin to understand his trading concept and define his win rate or probability for success. Then, I look at the profit column in order to define an average reward ratio for the client's trading strategy. With those two parameters in hand, I am in a position to run through the same mathematical process used to determine the edge in our coin flip or roulette examples used earlier in the text. With a baseline for profit expectation per trade established, I begin to examine the trading log in an attempt to find the payout/payback cycles. With the benefit of hindsight, these waves of red and black ink are usually easy to find. Once the sine wave of payout/payback is highlighted, then the real problem-solving process begins.

Identify Your Keystone Transition Event

Like the detective in a crime novel, I pour over the transition periods as the client's account cycles from payout to payback, then from payback into payout once again. I look for any clues contained within the trading results that might lead me to the *keystone* transition event. The keystone is a consistently repeated behavior/event that tends to precede a change in the clients payout/payback cycle. This keystone event will be different for every client, and for every trading strategy, but often can be identified by some of the following characteristics:

1. a change in trading frequency as the trader begins to over trade in reaction to frustrating market action,
2. the beginnings of a draw down,
3. simple mental exhaustion.

I continually find it amazing how often traders radically increase their aggressiveness or activity *just as the market environment turns against* their particular trading strategy! This leads to another common misconception about trading. The way to make more money as a trader is to increase risk and position size—PERIOD—END OF SENTENCE! So many traders incorrectly feel that if they "trade harder," or trade more markets, their profitability will increase. It has been my professional *and personal* experience, that traders actually experience an *increase* in edge and profitability as trading frequency *decreases*.

CHAPTER 3

SELECTIVE AGGRESSION

*I shall do less whenever I shall believe what I am doing hurts
the cause and I shall do more whenever I shall believe doing
more will help the cause. I shall try to correct errors when
shown errors and I shall adopt new views as fast as they
shall appear to be true views.*

—Abraham Lincoln

It has been my privilege over the years to meet some
of my heroes in the trading business. These are the people
who inspire me, and keep me going during the draw downs
and other painful experiences the market delivers to the
professional trader. When I first started in this business,
I, too, incorrectly believed that these traders made more money
than I did because they had some "secret" knowledge that
I lacked. I soon began to realize that while their experience
and research worked to deliver more edge than I might
currently be capturing, the reason they were able to take
millions of dollars out of the market each year was because of
their position size.

10K Rule

On a trade where I might have been risking $500 in an attempt to capture $1,500 in profits, these traders would be risking $15,000 in an attempt to make $45,000! It was from conversations and experiences with these market masters that I came up with what I term the "10K Rule." While this rule has proven to be quite controversial, I believe in it absolutely and have a great deal of anecdotal evidence from the clients in my consulting practice to back up its validity. The 10K Rule simply states,

> *For every $100 risked on an average trade, a skilled professional speculator should expect to realize approximately $10,000 in income per year.*

You can use this rule to reality test your income goals as a trader. Do you need to make $50,000 per year in order to replicate your current income? Then you will need the capital to appropriately risk $500 per trade over the course of the next year. Would you like to make $200,000 next year? Then you will need the trading capital to appropriately risk $2,000 per trade in the year to come. Therefore, if your goal is to make $1 million a year as a trader, you will need to risk at least $10,000 on each and every trade you take!

Trading at this level brings up a whole host of new mental challenges. Will you have the discipline to continue trading your strategy without error after taking a $50,000–$90,000 draw down over the course of a week? Will your eye and feel for the markets go cold when you are in the depths of a payback super cycle, and are looking at a $250,000 draw down? Will you get euphoric and sloppy after banking the profits on a position trade that delivered a $400,000 profit?

The guts and discipline you must have to take this level of monetary risk without losing objectivity or discipline is the major determinant between the moderately successful and superstar traders.

Sometimes the keystone event is contained in the number of winning trades contained in a given winning streak. For my equity swing trading strategies, the keystone is the fifth winning trade in a row. By looking at my historical returns, I have discovered that my profitability goes out the window shortly after any sustained five-trade winning streak. If I have just enjoyed a winning streak of this size, I know it is time to withdraw from the markets in order to protect my newly acquired profits. Conversely, my payback cycles tend to wear themselves out after six to eight losing trades. For this reason, even though I may choose not to take risk for several days after a sustained win streak, I am still watching the market as I count all losing trades I hope to be missing.

Because of the natural tendency to chase "hot" strategies, the first few signals of a new payout cycle tend to be the most profitable. Traders have yet to identify the pattern as being "hot," and therefore are slow to react to setups. Due to the recent payback environment, they tend to be trading from a place of mental frustration and anger. This leads to chasing and other sloppy behaviors that help to build the profits of the new payout cycle's early adopters. Because of this tendency, I begin trading again as soon as I see six losers come and go. I am often a little early, and will take one–three stop-losses on average as a result. But the extraordinarily large gains often seen in the first two trading signals of the new payout cycle more than offset these small draw downs. If I am too conservative, and wait for the new payout cycle to prove itself, I will have abdicated a great deal of edge that will really add up against me by the end of the trading year.

For some traders, their keystone events are based on elements of seasonality. I had one client whose consistent profitability in the fall and winter trading seasons degraded dramatically once spring had sprung. Year after year, this trader produced the bulk of his profits over a four to five month span, and essentially wasted his efforts the rest of the year. Whether this was due to some aspect of market seasonality, or simply the fact that his mental state suffered when it was nice outside and he was stuck behind his trading screens, I will never know. But after analyzing his trading programs, it was very clear to me as an outside observer that shutting down entirely from May/June to late September would sharply increase this client's overall profitability.

Your job as a professional speculator is like the doctor's oath: "first, do no harm." A good trader will find himself treading water for long periods of time when the market is not in alignment with his style. However, the benefits of this successful payback cycle analysis loses its meaning if you are unwilling to trade aggressively when the gains of the payout cycle present themselves once more. If you were to graph the equity curve of a profitable trader, you would see a consistent pattern of base, jump, base, jump, as their equity curve zigs and zags to new highs. The bulk of their gains will be realized in clusters as the sustained win streaks of their pay out cycles manifest themselves. I find that traders continually get mired in the morass of price pattern selection and identification. While these tasks help to develop edge, they do little to optimize it or help convert its statistical advantage into actual trading income. However, if you spend the majority of your analysis time optimizing your edge and looking for ways to minimize your draw downs through payout/payback cycle analysis, the benefits will be immediate and profound.

As with almost every aspect in trading, the appearance of edge can be deceiving. In my experience, the majority of traders spend far too much time constantly seeking ways to increase their accuracy or win/loss ratio. It "feels" better to trade when you have fewer losses to deal with, but ironically the most profitable trading strategies I have discovered all have abysmal win rates. These strategies are uncomfortable to trade because of the numerous small losses one must endure. However, the risk-to-reward ratio these strategies offer are so large that the end result is a much more profitable edge.

Risk-to-Reward Strategies

For the purposes of this exercise, we shall assume that both these trading strategies have withstood the test of time, and that their basic edge parameters are tested and trustworthy. These strategies will both be traded by a trader with a $100,000 account, who plans to risk $1,000 per trade.

Low Accuracy/Large Risk-to-Reward

The first strategy seeks to capture large trend reversals, and will fade into a rising or falling market once a day each time a potential top or bottom forms. Since this trading strategy enters at each potential reversal point, when any significant reversal occurs, the trader will realize an average gain of at least five to one. Since one is consistently taking positions against the trend, the downside of this strategy is its 25 percent to 30 percent win rate.

Results of a Low Accuracy/Large Risk-to-Reward Strategy

−$1,000	$5,000	−$1,000	$5,000	−$1,000
−$1,000	−$1,000	−$1,000	−$1,000	−$1,000
−$1,000	−$1,000	−$1,000	−$1,000	$7,000
−$1,000	−$1,000	−$1,000	−$1,000	$5,000

In this particular month, there were only four trades that produced a gain. In spite of the fact that the strategy under-performed as it only produced a 20 percent win rate for the month, it still managed to produce $6,000 in income. While on the face of it, a 6 percent per month return is more than accept-able, let us spend a moment looking at the emotional reality of trading this strategy through the month in question.

Figure 3.1 shows the equity curve for this trading strategy through the month in question. Starting with $100,000, the account quickly accumulates $9,000 in gains by the fourth trad-ing day of the month. Imagine how wonderfully euphoric you would feel to realize a 9 percent gain on your account in just a few days! Since our trader is aware of the existence of the pay-out/payback cycle, he understands that after such a quick and easy payout cycle, a period of adversity lies on the horizon. As powerful as the high of the previous euphoria might have been, it is quickly mirrored by a depressing and frustrating draw down. Ten losing trades in a row are seen in a payback cycle that takes the account from 9 percent up to 1 percent down for the month!

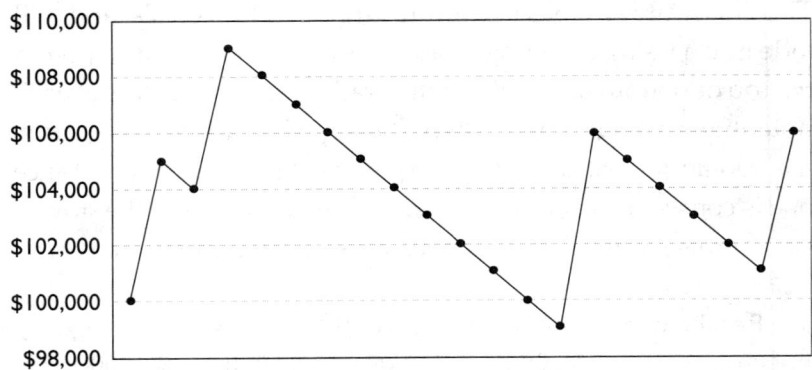

Figure 3.1

After this sustained losing streak, a larger than average profit is realized as the market finally turns and delivers the reversal that the strategy has been targeting all along. This puts the account back in the black, and justifies the multiple failed entries within the draw down period. The experience this example shows so far is how important it is to remain absolutely disciplined when trading a low accuracy trading style. Imagine if the trader had succumbed to the emotional discomfort of the draw down period, and had missed the above-average gain that followed. This one simple error would have cost the trader $7,000 in profits!

The rest of the month doesn't offer much to the trader. A small draw down cycle is followed by an average gain, and the strategy ends its month showing a 6 percent ($6,000) gain. Luck, and natural statistical variance delivered a slightly weak performance for the strategy this month. But even with only 20 percent of trades taken producing positive results, the strategy produced a solid 6 percent gain. Imagine if the pendulum swings the other direction, and you are trading the strategy during a month when it hits at 35 percent. Your expected gain would be a whopping 22 percent, or $22,000 in profit! The combined profits for this two-month period would then be 28 percent, a far from average return.

High Accuracy/Small Risk-to-Reward

The second strategy seeks to capture a small but consistent gain within the volatility that surrounds the opening of the stock market. Like the low accuracy/large risk reward strategy detailed earlier, this high accuracy/small risk reward strategy will risk $1,000 in an attempt to capture a one-to-one gain. One of the strategy's benefits is its 65 percent win rate, which ensures that a trader will be banking many more profits than losses.

High Accuracy/Small Risk-to-Reward Ratio Trading Strategy

$1,000	$1,000	$1,000	$1,000	$1,000
$1,000	−$1,000	−$1,000	$1,000	−$1,000
−$1,000	−$1,000	$1,000	−$1,000	−$1,000
$1,000	$1,000	$1,000	$1,000	−$1,000

In this particular month, there were 12 trades that produced a gain. Like the first strategy, this month's accuracy rate ran on the lean side at 60 percent due to luck and natural statistical variance. Again, even though the strategy underperformed slightly as it produced a 60 percent win rate for the month, it still produced $4,000 in income. Figure 3.2 shows the emotional reality of this trading strategy's equity curve for the month.

Starting with $100,000, the trader first experiences a strong payout cycle as six winning trades in a row are banked for a 6 percent gain. Any trader who was aware of the existence of the payout/payback cycle would be expecting a draw down after such a tremendous win streak. His analysis would have helped him save some money as the draw down arrived right on schedule. The losses from the payback cycle take the account back down near the break even point. However, the next payout cycle begins just before the $100,000 level is

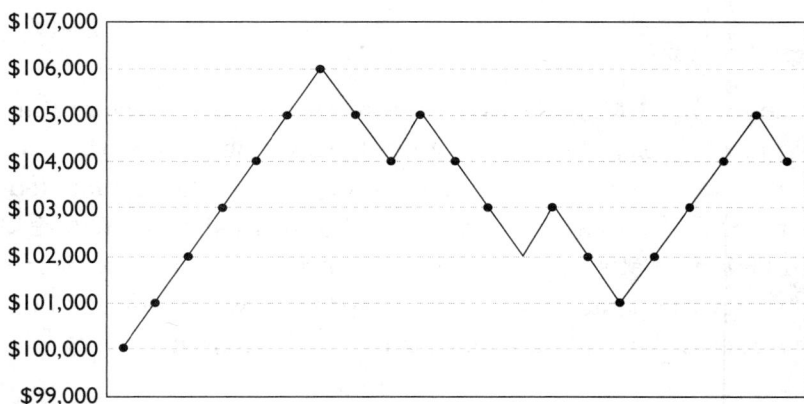

Figure 3.2

reached, and another solid five trade win streak forms. The month ends on a tiny down note, and this small loss brings the months total profit to $4,000.

Luck, and statistical variance delivered a slightly weak performance for the high accuracy/small risk reward strategy this month. But even with only 60 percent of trades producing positive results, the strategy produced a 4 percent gain. Again, imagine if the pendulum swings the other direction, and you are trading the strategy during a month when it hits at 70 percent. Your expected gain would be 8 percent, or $8,000 in profits. Therefore the combined profit for this two-month period would be 12 percent.

Can you detect a pattern here? Even though the majority of traders spend enormous amounts of time and money searching for ways to increase their accuracy, they fail to realize that they could dramatically increase their bottom line by focusing the same amount of energy on increasing their average risk-reward ratio! Even if these changes reduce the overall accuracy rate, the chances are high that the average profits at the end of the month will be dramatically higher. A trader must be willing to accept the more volatile equity curves that a low accuracy/high risk reward trading model delivers, but the added profitability at the end of each quarter should more than offset any mental stress.

I had a trader come to me during a sustained trading slump. While his trading was still nominally profitable, it wasn't enough to comfortably cover his monthly expenditures. Upon analyzing his recent track record, I realized that although his edge was valid, he was not demanding enough of a risk-to-reward ratio from his trades. Because of the stress involved in "trading for the rent" during a weakly profitable period, he had drifted toward a high accuracy management style. He had done a very good job at identifying important turning points in the

> market, but had opted to capture the quick and easy gains, rather than hold on for the profit potential of a larger move. His average risk reward ratio of one and a half to one wasn't getting the job done. (And more importantly, was not paying him the profits that his accurate market predictions deserved!)

I put together a package that compared his actual gains for the month with a trading model that demanded a three-to-one risk reward ratio before allowing profits to be taken. This management adjustment would have been difficult to implement, as a number of his trades that month had rallied close to the two to one level before failing. He would have watched several thousand dollars in profits vanish more than once, and it would have taken complete discipline not to allow these losses to affect his emotional stability.

But the mathematics of edge surrounding this management shift were powerful. Even though his accuracy rate would have suffered, the dramatic increase in average risk-to-reward ratio would have delivered more than three times the profitability he actually experienced. So essentially, I told him the market was offering him a choice: Trade as he did before, and sacrifice profitability for emotional comfort, or be willing to accept and ignore any discomfort surrounding a lower accuracy rate and triple his income. I'm happy to say he chose the latter, and saw his average monthly gain rise dramatically over the next quarter.

Your job as a trader, whether a hobbyist or full-time professional, is not to pick winning trades, but instead to pull profits out of the world's markets. As is often the case in this perverse business, the biggest edges and most dramatic profitability come from the low accuracy/high risk-to-reward trading strategies. I strongly suggest you ignore the false idols of accuracy and win rates, and put all of your time and focus during the strategy development process into extracting larger risk-to-reward ratios.

Exercises

Analyze the following trading logs using the worksheets provided in the appendixes and determine the following:

1. What is the accuracy rate of this sample?
2. What is the worst experienced draw down of the sample?
3. What is the average risk-to-reward ratio in the sample?
4. What is the average edge expressed in dollars per trade?
5. Is this a high accuracy/small risk reward, or low
   accuracy/high risk reward trading strategy?

Example 1	Example 2:	Example 3:	Example 4:
$900	$500	$125	$125
$500	$500	−$500	−$250
−$525	−$250	$750	$125
$1500	$500	$325	$250
−$500	−$262	−$562	−$250
−$500	$500	$125	−$250
$750	$500	$512	$125
$900	$500	−$300	$125
−$425	−$250	$139	$250
−$525	−$250	−$225	$250
$125	−$250	$289	−$250
$900	$500	−$725	$125
$350	$500	$83	$250
−$475	−$250	−$974	$250
$350	$500	$1200	$125
−$525	−$250	−$25	$125
−$500	−$250	$637	−$250
$1200	−$250	−$625	$125
$350	−$250	$350	$125
−$500	$500	−$600	−$250

CHAPTER 4

DEVELOPING A BUSINESS PLAN

You've got to be very careful if you don't know where you're going, because you might not know when you get there!

—YOGI BERRA

Now that you understand the process used to determine the statistical probabilities for any given trading strategy's success, you are in a position to begin developing an executable trading plan. Any edge is little more then a theoretical possibility until you prove that profits can realistically be captured in a real-world trading environment. Without a robust and properly developed trading plan, there is little chance for you to realize the true profit potential of any given market edge.

What Is Discipline?

The word "discipline" is overused to the point of abuse in the literature on trading. For many, the word means having the fortitude to take a loss when a trade is going against you. I take this ability as a given. It is a simple fact that any trader who succumbs to "blowing stops," doubling down on bad positions in an attempt to get even, or other suicidal money-management errors will not survive long enough to ever become a blip on anyone's radar. The word discipline to me means standing by the rules of the trading plan that created a positive expectancy during the strategy generation/analysis process. If you are planning to back a trading strategy with actual risk capital, then you should have already gone through all the testing phases to determine whether true profitability exists before putting any real dollars at risk.

I have yet to discover a profitable trading concept that did not deliver periods of extreme mental stress and discomfort. These uncomfortable periods are universal to the speculative trading experience, and should be anticipated and accepted as unavoidable. When you are experiencing emotional discomfort, it is often tempting to deviate from your trading plan in order to make yourself "feel better" by removing the object of irritation. While this natural reaction helps to protect you in the physical world when you touch a hot pan, it will work *against you* in the world of speculation.

There is an old market adage that states: "when you look at your position and feel like vomiting, DOUBLE YOUR POSITION!" While I don't have a double down policy in many of my trading plans, I totally believe in the concept behind this statement. When your mental pain due to losses, or the fear of loss is at its most extreme, the market will often be offering its largest rewards. To succeed as a trader, you must accept that losses are an expected and constant aspect of this business. You can expect that they will occur regularly, and without predictability within the context of any trading strategies payout/payback cycle. Once you accept and internalize this market reality, you will move to a place of mental objectivity that will help you keep from personalizing your losses.

When we first begin to trade, it is universal to assume that every loss occurs because of a mistake or a lack of information on our part. Each loss feels like a personal failure, a slap on the wrist from the market gods. Only through time, experience, and education does one thoroughly understand the payout/payback cycle, and its manic-depressive hero to zero cyclicality.

The longer you trade, the more wacky war stories you will have to tell: the trade that missed your exit point by one cent, then tanked and triggered your break-even stop; the trade that only filled you partially, and delivered $500 in profits instead of the $5,000 you expected; the trade you held patiently for weeks until your predetermined time stop triggered, THEN rallied right up to your profit objective. All these scenarios can cause a great deal of consternation and mental distress. But in each instance, since you managed the trade exactly according to your predefined plan, these losses were not due to any error on your part.

These frustrating trades are "good trades" with a bad outcome. Accepting that there will be a number of good trades with bad outcomes such as these is mandatory if you wish to achieve consistent profitability. You cannot allow these instances of bad luck to provoke errors in management in the trades that are to follow.

Your research should have indicated what tools/rules you will be using to define your stop-loss level for each position. Hopefully, during the research and edge development/analysis process, you will have developed a significant level of trust and confidence in your edge. Having the discipline to hold your stops no matter what is based on faith that your trading plan is robust and well developed. Again and again, I have taken trades that felt like total failures. Immediately after entry, they went against me and stayed underwater sometimes for days. I would've bet you any amount of money that it was just a matter of time before the stop-loss levels were triggered, yet these trades eventually reversed without warning and ended up reaching their profit objectives!

Pick Stop-loss Levels, Carefully

There is a strong mental urge, to "cut your losses and run" when a trade doesn't immediately show you some reward after entry. But in order to ever achieve profitability as a trader, you must have the discipline to pick your stop-loss levels carefully and not "jump" those stops. Ironically, although it "feels" like the safe and right thing to do, failing to hold stops is an incredibly destructive behavior that will significantly damage one's overall edge. Exiting trades early without giving them a chance to pay off dooms you to the death of a thousand cuts. Granted, you will never experience many large losses, but by giving up on your trades while they remain in their infancy, you never capture the large profits needed to offset the constant stream of small "controlled" losses that stop jumpers incur. Because of this shift in your risk-to-reward ratios, stop jumping is perhaps the most destructive behavior at trader can fall victim to.

Two traders discover a trading opportunity for the following day. The trade takes place in the equities market, and appears to offer $1.30 in profit potential for a $.38 risk. Both traders buy 2,500 shares, and begin managing their positions. Joe sets a stop market order to sell the position in full if the market trades $.38 below entry. Once the order is live, he turns back to his desk and begins to finish up some paperwork that needs attention. Harry initiates a similar stop-loss order, and begins watching intently as he actively manages the trade. By the end of the morning session, the stock has done little to justify its existence. Volume has been light, and both positions are approximately $.20 below break even. Joe is unaffected by this lack of performance, as his trading plan is based on price, not time. Harry is frustrated by the stocks lack of reaction, and decides to scratch the position if it remains underwater after lunch. At 1:00 P.M.., the position is still $.18 below the break even point, so Harry scratches the position for a smaller than expected $450 loss. The stock closes weakly, and Harry feels justified in his exit.

The next morning the stock gaps up at the open, and begins to trend in earnest. By the end of the session, it has rallied nearly 2 points, and has met the initial profit objective for the trade. Joe maintained his discipline and did not deviate from his trading plan, and as a result realizes a profit of $3,250. ($1.30 × 2,500 shares) Harry's decision to scratch the trade has cost him enormously. With an initial position size of 2,500 shares, Harry was risking $750 on this trade. Harry believed at the time he scratched the trade that failure was imminent, and that by scratching he was "saving" himself $300. Harry thus abdicated his right to any future profits by allowing his fear of loss to drive him to jump his stop. In actuality this decision "cost" Harry $3,700! He lost $450 in actual capital, and $3,250 in unrealized profits. If Harry's next trade produces another $750 stop-loss, then he will be down more than $1,000 for the month. In sharp contrast, if Joe's next trade is a $750 loser, his tally sheet will show a $2,500 profit for the month. The importance of this "spread risk" between theoretical edge and real-world execution cannot be over emphasized. It is often the reason that clients come to my consulting practice looking for help. They have a valid edge, but are actually doing more monetary damage to their returns by jumping stops then picking bad trades! In the example above, Harry's decision to scratch the trade early cost him almost *5 times his normal stop size.*

He could have committed every rookie mistake possible, and would have had to pick five terrible trades in a row in order to do the same amount of monetary damage to his bottom line. So do the research needed to become confident in your edge, and don't start trading with real money until you have fully committed yourself to the trading plan that has proven on paper to be profitable.

Determine Your Correct Level of Dollar Risk

Once you are committed to following the rules of your trading plan, you are ready to determine the correct level of dollar risk for your account. Look at the average draw down for the trading strategy you are about to implement, and use this information to determine the appropriate level of dollar risk per trade. A good rule of thumb that I use regarding success is to take the worst experienced draw down and triple it. In other words, a strategy would have to experience its worst draw down ever *three consecutive times* in order to bankrupt the account. In all my years as a trader, I have yet to experience three full draws in a row in any trading strategy. This triple draw down method determines the worst likely draw down, and gives you a level to work from to analyze your "risk of ruin." If your research indicates that the worst experienced draw down for the trading strategy question was 7 units, then a 21 unit draw down becomes your position sizing standard.

I have long used a "unit" based sizing strategy for all of my trading programs. This concept handicaps the volatility of any trading instrument and allows me to compare apples to oranges with total accuracy. Each losing trade, no matter how large or small the stop-loss may be, will cost me approximately the same amount in real dollars lost. If my "unit size" is $1,000, I will scale my position size so that a $3 loss in an equities position trade, or a five tick loss in the S&P futures, will both cost me $1,000.

This position sizing strategy balances all my trading programs against one another, and allows me to easily determine my performance for any given day/week/month. If I take a trade in the currency markets, and it produces a three unit gain, while at the same time a swing trade in the stock of IBM fails and produces a one unit loss than my net profit for the day is two units. The algorithm used for this position sizing methodology is very simple:

Dollars to be risked / Size of the stop in dollars

For example, if you decide to risk $350 on an equities trade with a $2.50 stop-loss, 140 shares would be purchased. If you wished to risk the same $350 on a trade in the Dow Mini Futures with a 10 pip stop-loss, then a 7 contract position would be established. As a rule of thumb, I find that most day trading strategies produce 10 to 20 units of profit during their payout cycles, and 5 to 10 units of loss during payback. Personally, I don't care to expose myself to more than a 10 percent draw down on my equity in a given month, so I tend to risk $1/4$ percent to $1/2$ percent on my intra day positions. If I have a bad day and take two stop-losses, my account will be down approximately $1/2$ percent My swing trading strategies tend to produce five to eight units of profit in payout, three to five units of draw down when in payback. Because of this, I tend to size my swing trades for a 1 percent risk.

Build Your Trading Plan

Once you have defined your strategy's edge, and have determined what your standard position (unit size) will be, you are ready to begin writing your trading plan. Like any business, developing a game plan before strategy implementation will give you a structure to fall back on any time you feel unsure about a management choice due to market generated emotionality. There is a fallacy among beginning traders that the professional speculator is an emotionless robot executing trades perfectly without the stresses and frustrations that trading can generate. Nothing could be further from the truth! Every market participant rides the roller coaster from payout to pay back, hero to zero. The difference is that those of us with experience understand intimately the emotional traps the market sets for us. Rather than reacting incorrectly to emotional pain, we exploit these negative feelings as contrary indicators in our own trading.

Building a trading plan is similar to the process a football team goes through when scrimmaging. It provides the opportunity to build a structure for success that can be relied on during times of extreme adversity or stress. When you build your trading plan, you are working from a totally objective place. You have no positions and therefore you have no emotional or monetary investment in bullish or bearish arguments. As soon as you pull the trigger, you are emotionally and monetarily enslaved to that particular market. The inexperienced trader lives and dies with every tick, and more often than not commits emotionally based blunder after blunder as the market charts its drunken path from one point to another.

Prepare for Adverse Market Conditions

A robust trading plan will have the answer on how to react to just about every market situation possible. When the going gets tough, the time spent preparing your response to adverse situations will save you thousands of dollars. I have yet to live through a year of trading without at least one major crisis to react/defend/respond to.

To help you build your trading plan, read through the following list of questions and answer them in detail:

- Describe and define your edge. What are the setups? What market behaviors will you use to develop your market bias?
- How will the market be required to act in order to trigger your buy and sell signals?
- What tactics and/or order types will you use to enter and exit your trades?
- What rules will you use to determine where stop-loss orders should be set?
- What tools, methods, and strategy will you use in order to find these setups?
- Will you trade the strategy in only one time frame?
- Is this a strategy that you will trade to the short side as well as the long?
- What are your strategies for taking profits?
- What keystone events will you use to determine when you are in the transition zone from payout to payback?
- What keystone events will you use to determine when you are in the transition zone from payback to payout?
- What changes will you make to your position management strategy after you have identified that you are trading within the context of a payout cycle?
- What changes will you make to your position management strategy after you have identified that you are trading within the context of a payback cycle?
- How much money are you willing to lose during the course of a normal draw down before you cease trading operations and re-examine your edge?
- How much money are you willing to lose in a month before you cease trading operations and re-examine your edge?
- Define what types of failure you might see that would make you consider abandoning this strategy?

Once you have answered all these questions in detail, you will have created a robust and comprehensive trading plan. The goal should be to have a plan that is clear and explicit enough that some third party could understand it and manage your open trades for you. Use this plan as a crutch when you are feeling frustrated and angry, and stick to its instructions with absolute rigidity and discipline.

Follow Your Plan

Having taken the time to think about trade failure and how best to manage it, you will be in a position to read and follow your written instructions when you are in your least objective mindset. During a period of draw down, peruse your trading plan to see if the current level of losses is within the normal draw down parameters.

I am often surprised at the number of traders who come to my consulting practice looking for help simply because

Insider's Advice If your trading results are substandard, you can double check to make sure that you are following all the rules contained within your trading plan. If you trade your plan, and fail to make money, then you know that the underperformance is the plan's "fault," and not some error you have committed. If you know the rules have been followed, then you are in a position to begin analyzing your strategy's edge to see if the market has shifted away from the behaviors that made it initially profitable. If you do not have the clear knowledge that it is *the plan* that failed, then there is no way to determine *where* to begin analysis in order to restore profitability. The failure could be some error you are committing, a flaw in the trade management tactics, or simply that the market environment has changed. Without a trade plan in place, you will have no way to know.

they are failing to execute their own self-generated trading plans. Their initial edge is usually valid, but they never experienced the profitability that their edge deserves because they failed to follow their trading plan's parameters.

CHAPTER 5

EXPLOITING YOUR EDGE

Failure is simply the opportunity to begin again, this time more intelligently.

—HENRY FORD

By observing the many traders I've worked with over the years, I have identified the top five reasons traders fail to capture the profits their strategies should be producing:

1. lack of, or a poorly written plan,
2. consistently taking profits that have failed to justify their risk,
3. inappropriate sizing of positions,
4. inability to accept market risk, and
5. lack of consistent approach to the market.

Poorly Written Trading Plan

The primary reason that traders lose money is the lack of, or a poorly written trading plan. As we have explored in the previous chapter, the trading plan is your blueprint for success. A well-developed trading plan will guide your actions through the troubled times of the payback cycle and help keep you from becoming foolishly optimistic during the final days of the payout cycle.

Taking Small Profits and Large Losses

The second most common reason that traders fail is that they consistently take profits that failed to justify their initial risk. They jump stops, take profits too soon, and generally decimate their strategy's edge by consistently taking small profits, and large losses (instead of the other way around). This inverts the power of the risk-to-reward ratio that a low probability/high risk reward delivers and just about guarantees underperformance and loss. Over the years as I have tried to steer my clients away from this common error, I developed what I term the "minimum profit objective" or MPO. The minimum profit objective is defined as the point at which your open profits justify the initial risk of the trade. You can use the following formulaic example to determine the MPO for any particular trading strategy.

(100 − (Win Rate)) / Win Rate

If we run this equation on a trading strategy with a win rate of 45 percent, you can see that this strategy would need to have its MPO at 1.2 to 1.

100 − 45 = 55 and 55 / 45 = 1.222

In order for this trading strategy to break even at its current win rate, a minimum of 1.2 to 1 is needed. If 100 trades are taken, 45 should result in a profitable outcome, while 55 will produce a loss. If you risk $100 and demand at least $120 in profits, then the losing trades will produce $5,500 (55 × 100). The profits from the winning trades at the MPO will almost exactly offset these losses $5,400 (45 × 120).

If a trading idea has a 29 percent win rate, then the MPO would be as follows:

$$100 - 29 = 71 \text{ and } 71 / 29 = 2.44$$

If 100 trades are taken, this trading strategy should produce a profitable outcome 29 times. The remaining 71 trades would produce losses. If you risk $100 and demand at least $244 in profits, then the losing trades will produce $7,100 (71 × 100). The profits from the winning trades at the MPO will almost exactly offset these losses $7,076 (29 × 244).

Inappropriate Sizing of Positions

The third most common trading error I have observed is the inappropriate sizing of positions. Because of the emotional triggers that the payout/payback cycle generate, traders often feel compelled to take large positions at the most inappropriate moments possible. The size of your positions should be determined by the size of your average draw down, and the amount of money *in actual dollars* that you are willing to lose on this trading program. A deeper discussion of this topic will follow shortly, but I have seen a number of traders cut short a quite promising

Insider's Advice As you can see from the examples I've shown, a trader cannot *mathematically afford* to take a profit that is less than the MPO; to do so will put him in a negative expectancy situation. While this is a very simple concept, few traders seem to fully understand the damage your edge will suffer if MPO levels are ignored.

career because they impulsively changed their position sizes to a level that made the risk of ruin a possible if not probable event.

Inability to Accept Market Risk

The fourth most common trading error is simply the inability to accept market risk. Ironically, this trading error is seen most frequently in traders with only a little, or a great deal of experience. The beginners don't understand edge as well as they should, and as a result are afraid of losses. They take each loss is a personal failure, something they could avoid "if they just study a little bit harder." The experienced trader often falls victim to this negative trading behavior after a sharp increase in size amplified the emotional swings of their payout/payback cycles. The majority of the experienced clients I have worked with on this problem had been successful trading their own money, but once they started to manage money for others, the size of the risk involved twisted their emotions. Instead of risking $1,000 on a trade, now they were risking $20,000, and the amount of money involved put them far outside their comfort zone.

As with most trading errors, the inability to accept risk can be addressed with a clear and robust trading plan. After all, the market doesn't care whether you are trading 100, 1000, or 10,000 shares … only *you* do! One of the beautiful things about speculation as a business is its nearly infinite scalability. With most business models, growth is a process of physical construction, human resources development, and supply chain growth. To grow a speculative business, all you need to do is add a few zeros to your position size and your business can double or triple overnight. If you have just recently increased your level of risk, and are experiencing a degradation in return, think long and hard about the true nature of your risk acceptance. Often this one little error is the root of all your evils!

Lack of Consistent Approach to the Market

The fifth and final reason why many traders fail to make money is due to their lack of consistent approach to their markets. This error, like stop jumping seems innocuous enough on the face of it. The trader is working through his/her learning curve, and is trying to gain as much education and experience as is possible in a short period of time. They try 40 different trading styles, with 40 different position management strategies, and as a result interact daily with 40 different payout/payback cycles. On Monday, they trade the signals from one or two strategies, on Tuesday they try a few signals from a few more. Not surprisingly, this randomness of approach breeds a randomness of result, and can lead to erroneous assumptions about the profitability of any given edge.

On one day due to blind luck, you will trade a strategy that is in the midst of a payout cycle, and the positive feedback you receive will make you think this strategy is the cat's pajamas. The next day, again solely due to luck, you will take the setups from a strategy in the midst of a payback cycle, and the negative feedback you receive will cause you to abandon what could otherwise be an extremely profitable setup.

Insider's Advice Until you have observed and traded a strategy through at least one full payout/payback cycle, you lack the information needed to make a clear projection about an edge's potential profitability. Granted, it does take time and effort to correctly analyze a new edge, but once you have enough data to accurately predict the size and duration of the average payout/payback cycle you are in a position to use leverage to scale your position size in order to meet your performance goals.

Exploit Your Strategy's Edge

Now that you have an understanding of how to analyze any potential trading strategy for edge, and a working knowledge of some of the primary mistakes that traders make that sabotage that edge, you are in a position to begin honing your basic trading plan to most efficiently exploit your strategy's edge. At the outset, one must define what your investment goals are. If the goal is to build wealth slowly and steadily within a retirement account, then the appropriate level of risk and acceptable draw down will be much smaller than the income generating account of a professional trader.

Leverage

Leverage refers to the use of borrowed money to increase the potential return of any financial investment. The ability to borrow differs with each financial instrument, and while one can spend a great deal of time on this subject, my years of experience have let me boil it down to one simple truth—I have yet to trade a market or an instrument that *failed to offer me the leverage I needed* to trade effectively. Every market, every instrument I have used as a speculative instrument has always offered me more than enough leverage to do the job. Yet I find that traders continually operate under the mistaken belief that more buying power makes an instrument better somehow.

While at its root it is true that more leverage can mean more income potential, more leverage also delivers an equal amount of increased risk. Think of leverage as a volume knob that can turn a trading strategy with an average monthly profit of $2,000 and average draw down of $1,000 into a trading strategy with an average monthly profit of $6,000 and an average draw down of $3,000. The rhythm of the "music" is the same; all you have done is increase the "volume" of the profit and loss columns.

Having analyzed a trading strategy's edge, and historical draw down tendencies during its payback cycles, you will be in a position to accurately assess your "risk of ruin" at any particular level of leverage. This is why I developed the three times average draw down as my rule of thumb for defining position size. Once I have established what I believe to be the appropriate level of dollar risk per trade, I ignore the leverage and simply execute the trades as dictated by my trading plan. Leverage becomes just another tool my trading business needs in order to function.

Add to Open Positions

When some discuss leverage, in reality they are describing the process of adding to open positions or "pyramiding" using open profits. Adding exposure can be an incredibly destructive behavior if done on an unplanned reactionary basis. The trading adage "losers average losers" deals with the tendency for emotionally driven traders to inappropriately use leverage and add exposure to their failing positions. In a vain attempt to bolster their returns and get back to break even, these traders actually set themselves up for disaster. By using emotions to determine when to add, they guarantee that their largest positions will be established on their weakest trades. They are turning up their volume knob to "11" just as the music starts to feed back. The resultant leveraged howl of destruction blows up their account just as it might blow out the speakers of an amplifier.

Imagine that you've built a trading plan around buying stocks as they test a certain type of support. Your historical trade analysis has determined that a majority of these positions tend to reverse cleanly once support is tested. By measuring the average negative excursion of these tests, you determine that a $.50 stop-loss level should deliver you a 57 percent accuracy rate for this trade. However, once in a great while, support will be retested and a double bottom reversal pattern will form. These situations, although rare produce nearly twice the average follow—through, and therefore justify some additional risk exposure. Pyramiding *can* be a powerful tool if applied as part of a predetermined trading plan.

Insider's Advice   When double bottoms show themselves, plan to exploit the additional edge by doubling your position size. Although you will lose twice as much if these retest positions fail, you will capture nearly six times your average gain when they succeed! Thus, the decision to add exposure is correctly based on mathematical and statistical reality, rather than the emotionally based wish to wriggle out of a losing position.

Allow yourself to be open to the possibility of adding to your positions when secondary price action offers an enhanced risk-to-reward scenario, or confirms your original position. Adding correctly (in this manner) to positions increases your exposure to trades that are working in your favor, and can radically increase your average monthly gain. I tend to treat each add point as a separate trade nested within the original position. While most of the time these secondary entries share the same protective stop-loss level, in certain situations, these additional positions will have entirely different stop loss level and profit objectives.

Over time I have proven that I can correctly pick the bottom by "feel" after a sharp intraday sell-off has occurred in the S&P futures. By watching the tape, I try to identify when the selling reaches an extreme, and then take my entry. My trading history reveals that these entries are accurate to within two S&P points. If the market goes against my position more than two points, then my reversal opinion has been proven wrong, and the market is likely to go much lower. Every so often, I time the market perfectly, and achieve an extraordinarily accurate entry. My position is taken a tick or two off the lows of the day as the market makes a perfect "V" bottom. When this price action occurs, I can reduce my stop size to half its original level, (one point) and double my position size. Because of the sharply reduced stop-loss level, my net exposure for the trade remains nearly the same. This adding strategy, or *nested trade,* essentially doubles my upside potential while maintaining my original dollar levels of risk. By observing how the market reacts after offering me a buy signal, I have established a method to optimize and enhance my edge on a pre-existing trading strategy.

In Figure 5.1, I felt that the S&P had reached an area of support as it tested the 1520 area. The S&P E-Mini contract is worth $50 a point per contract, so with my initial two point stop-loss I was risking $100 per contract traded. Since I wanted to risk $1,000 on this trade, I took 10 contracts at 1520 (1), and set my stop-loss two points lower at 1518 (2). As luck would have it, my entry proved to be a very good one. The market went against me just three quarters of a point, and then bounced. I felt sure that this was the bounce move I had been targeting, so I felt I was in a position to trail my stop up one point, thus "saving" myself $500 in risk exposure (3). I decided to "nest" this trade, and so added to the position at the 1520.25 level. With my protective stop-loss trailed up to the 1519 area, this new position exposed me to a stop-loss exposure of 1.25 points

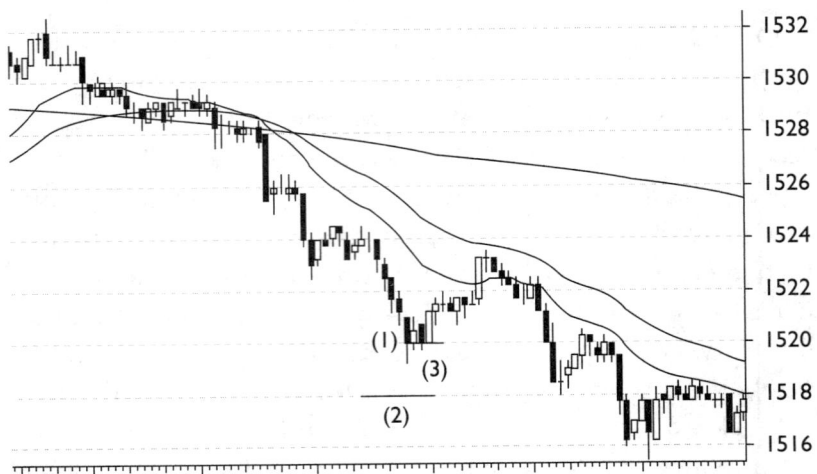

Figure 5.1 Example of a nested trade in the S&P 300 E-Mini

in size ($62.50 per contract). Since I had "saved" myself $500 on my initial position by trailing my stop, I now wished to add this risk back into the nested position. Therefore I sized my secondary position at eight contracts, (8 × $62.50 = $500 and in doing so brought my total exposure to the trade back to the $1,000 level. The market rallied up into an area of chart resistance near 1523, and I took my profits on both lots. So on my initial position I risked $1,000, and captured $1,500 (3 points of profit times 10 contracts.) for a risk-to-reward ratio of 1.5 to 1. My second lot had an initial risk of $500, and captured $1,100 (2.75 points of profit times 8 contracts.) for a risk-to-reward ratio of 2.2 to 1.

Taken as a whole, I was never exposed to more then a $1,000 loss, and yet was able to pull in a total of $2,600 in profits. The nested trade concept nearly doubled my risk-to-reward ratio *without taking any additional risk to capital!* This adding system leverages the luck and skill of an excellent entry to maximize your profits. These low tick entries are one of the hallmarks of a payout environment, and the nested trade concept is another way to leverage up the profit potential of these money making periods.

Developing a Trading Program for Wealth Generation

Another aspect of compounding can occur as profits accumulate in one's trading account over time. If you are trading for a living, then you will find that the majority of your profits will be drawn off as salary for living expenses. However, if an account's primary goal is wealth generation, then you will find that profit compounding is an important part of your overall trading plan. Since the average and worst experienced draw downs are components of all my trading plans, I use these parameters to calculate my profit compounding strategies as well.

Assume that an account is opened with the initial investment of $50,000, and that every month you invest an additional $500 from your other streams of income. Since this account's focus is wealth generation over time, you wish to keep the average draw down around 5 percent. Since our swing trading model has performed well over a number of years, you trust that its performance will continue. It tends to produce five to eight units of profit on average per month, with an average draw down of five units. It's worst time experienced draw down was 12 units, so as previously discussed, we will triple that and base our initial position sizing around a 36 unit disaster draw down scenario. The maximum draw down I am willing to risk on this account is 35 percent, or $17,500. $17,500 divided by 36 (Worst case experienced draw down tripled) gives us a basic unit size of $486. We will round that up to an even $500, and use that as our initial risk on every trade. Therefore, with a $500 unit size, we can project that this trading strategy will produce $2,500 to $4,000 in profit each month, with an average draw down of $2,500 (5 percent of initial starting capital). We will recalculate our position size using this same process each month, expanding our risk per trade as the account grows. If we follow this account's progress over the course of several years trading, we will see a very typical speculative experience. (See Table 5.1)

Table 5.1 Profit and loss data—years one and two

	Account	Unit P/L	Unit Size	P&L	$ added
Month 1	$50,000	6	500	$3,000	500
Month 2	$53,500	2	520	$1,040	500
Month 3	$55,040	4	535	$2,140	500
Month 4	$57,680	−8	560	−$4,480	500
Month 5	$53,700	11	525	$5,775	500
Month 6	$59,975	7	585	$4,095	500
Month 7	$64,570	1	625	$625	500
Month 8	$65,695	4	640	$2,560	500
Month 9	$68,755	3	670	$2,010	500
Month 10	$71,265	6	700	$4,200	500
Month 11	$75,965	1	740	$740	500
Month 12	$77,205	4	750	$3,000	500
		41		$24,705	
Month 1	$80,705	5	785	$3,925	500
Month 2	$85,130	6	825	$4,950	500
Month 3	$90,580	4	880	$3,520	500
Month 4	$94,600	7	925	$6,475	500
Month 5	$101,575	−3	985	−$2,955	500
Month 6	$99,120	−5	965	−$4,825	500
Month 7	$94,795	1	925	$925	500
Month 8	$96,220	−4	935	−$3,740	500
Month 9	$92,980	5	900	$4,500	500
Month 10	$97,980	7	950	$6,650	500
Month 11	$105,130	3	1,025	$3,075	500
Month 12	$108,705	8	1,050	$8,400	500
Total	$117,105	75		$55,605	

The first month is a good one, and six units of profit are captured. Using the same formula as before, ($53,500 × .35) our 35 percent draw down for this month would be $18,725. $18,550 divided by 36 gives us a unit size of $520 for the second month. This month generates only two units of profit, and produces a total profit of $1,040. Once again, we determine the maximum level of draw down, and calculate our position size for the upcoming month.

$$\$55,040 \times .35 = \$19,264 / 36 = \$535$$

The process repeats each month as the position size expands or contracts based on the account's starting equity for the month. At the end of the first year, a total of 41 units of profit have been captured. At this level of profit, with a fixed position size of $500, the trading program would have yielded $20,500 for the year. But by compounding profits and scaling position size on a monthly basis, we were able to capture an additional $4,700 and thus expand our profitability by more than 20 percent.

By the end of the second year, our $50,000 account has more than doubled to $117,000. And if we continue to model this trading program for 10 years, by the 10th year we have traded the account into the seven digits. (See Table 5.2)

Table 5.2 Profit and loss data—year ten

	Account Value	Unit P/L	Unit Size	P&L	$ added
Month 1	$998,875	−4	9,711	−$38,845	500
Month 2	$960,530	9	9,338	$84,046	500
Month 3	$1,045,076	2	10,160	$20,321	500
Month 4	$1,065,897	5	10,363	$51,814	500
Month 5	$1,118,212	−4	10,872	−$43,486	500
Month 6	$1,075,226	11	10,454	$114,989	500
Month 7	$1,190,715	−5	11,576	−$57,882	500
Month 8	$1,133,333	6	11,019	$66,111	500
Month 9	$1,199,944	1	11,666	$11,666	500
Month 10	$1,212,110	−8	11,784	−$94,275	500
Month 11	$1,118,335	11	10,873	$11,600	500
Month 12	$1,238,435	5	12,040	$60,202	500
Total	$1,299,137	29			

Over the course of this 10 year period, approximately 325 units of profit were captured. With a fixed $500 unit size, this comes out to $162,500 or a 325 percent return at the end of 10 years. Compare this outcome to $1,249,000 in profits (2,498 percent return) from the compounded program during the same period and you'll see how important it is to continually adjust your risk parameters as your account grows over time!

One last item to note is how the consistency of approach allowed the trading program in this example to grow steadily over time. The more consistent your average draw downs are, the more aggressive you can be without assuming an inappropriate risk of ruin. To better lock in these concepts, let us run through one more trading program. This time we will look at a trading plan with a much more aggressive approach.

Unlike the last example, this trading program is intended to produce monthly income by trading the foreign exchange markets. With an initial investment of $25,000, we are willing to lose every penny in the account, so will use leverage to maximize the profit potential of this strategy. Because of the leverage available to currency traders, we estimate that we could lose close to 75 percent of the account's value without having to compromise on position size. With an average maximum draw down of 10 units, the position sizing algorithm is as follows.

$$\$25,000 \times .75 = \$18,750 / 30 = \$625$$

Because the goal for this trading program is monthly income, we will take half the profits from every positive week as our salary. If the week's trading produces a loss, no salary will be paid. With these operating parameters, a typical year for this trading program might look like Table 5.3.

At the end of the year, the account has only gained $5,000 in value, but you would have earned a total of $105,000 in "salary."

Table 5.3 Trading for income—profit and loss data

	Account	Unit P/L	Unit Size	P&L	Salary
Week 1	$25,000	7	625	$4,375	$2,188
Week 2	$27,188	−6	680	−$4,078	$0
Week 3	$23,109	18	578	$10,399	$5,200
Week 4	$28,309	15	708	$10,616	$5,308
Week 5	$33,617	17	840	$14,287	$7,144
Week 6	$40,761	16	1019	$16,304	$8,152
Week 7	$48,913	−10	1223	−$12,228	$0
Week 8	$36,684	18	917	$16,508	$8,254
Week 9	$44,938	−10	1123	−$11,235	$0
Week 10	$33,704	8	843	$6,741	$3,370
Week 11	$37,074	−9	927	−$8,342	$0
Week 12	$28,733	−3	718	−$2,155	$0
Week 13	$26,578	6	664	$3,987	$1,993
Week 14	$28,571	−7	714	−$5,000	$0
Week 15	$23,571	1	589	$589	$295
Week 16	$23,866	13	597	$7,756	$3,878
Week 17	$27,744	−8	694	−$5,549	$0
Week 18	$22,195	7	555	$3,884	$1,942
Week 19	$24,137	14	603	$8,448	$4,224
Week 20	$28,361	−6	709	−$4,254	$0
Week 21	$24,107	−9	603	−$5,424	$0
Week 22	$18,683	−5	467	−$2,335	$0
Week 23	$16,348	14	409	$5,722	$2,861
Week 24	$19,208	15	480	$7,203	$3,602
Week 25	$22,810	11	570	$6,272	$3,136
Week 26	$25,946	−1	649	−$649	$0
Week 27	$25,297	12	632	$7,589	$3,795
Week 28	$29,092	15	727	$10,910	$5,455
Week 29	$34,547	−9	864	−$7,773	$0

(Continued)

Table 5.3 Trading for income—profit and loss data (Continued)

	Account	Unit P/L	Unit Size	P&L	Salary
Week 30	$26,774	12	669	$8,032	$4,016
Week 31	$30,790	2	769	$1,540	$769
Week 32	$31,560	−9	788	−$7,101	$0
Week 33	$24,459	9	611	$5,503	$2,752
Week 34	$27,210	1	680	$680	$340
Week 35	$27,551	4	688	$2,755	$1,378
Week 36	$28,928	8	723	$5,786	$2,893
Week 37	$31,821	1	795	$796	$398
Week 38	$32,219	5	805	$4,027	$2,014
Week 39	$34,232	−6	855	−$5,135	$0
Week 40	$29,098	4	727	$2,910	$1,455
Week 41	$30,552	11	763	$8,402	$4,201
Week 42	$34,753	2	868	$1,738	$869
Week 43	$35,622	−6	890	−$5,343	$0
Week 44	$30,279	−7	756	−$5,299	$0
Week 45	$24,980	−5	624	−$3,123	$0
Week 46	$21,858	11	546	$6,011	$3,005
Week 47	$24,863	16	621	$9,945	$4,976
Week 48	$29,836	1	745	$746	$373
Week 49	$30,208	−5	755	−$3,776	$0
Week 50	$26,432	5	660	$3,304	$1,652
Week 51	$28,084	−2	702	−$1,404	$0
Week 52	$26,680	11	667	$7,337	$3,669
Totals	$30,349				$105,551

Insider's Advice All you need to establish an edge in the marketplace is predictability and a strong risk-to-reward ratio. Develop edges built around the market open, edges built around the market close, edges built around seasonal tendencies, monthly tendencies, and the relationships between stocks in similar sectors; use edges built around esoteric mathematical principles and even edges based on astrological cycles! All of these diverse trading strategies share the same principles of preplanned trade management, and the ability to capture much more money on the reward side than one's initial risk.

If you were to project the result for this trading program over three years, you would see that the trading account has only grown to approximately $60,000, but you would have earned more than $400,000 over the course of the three years. These two examples show the difference between wealth generation and income generation as it pertains to program development. Over the long term, income generation programs will pay the bills, but will never make you rich! It is only once you are able to begin compounding your profits 100 percent that you may begin to pyramid your profits into "big money" over the course of several years.

CHAPTER 6

TRADER, SPECULATOR, OR INVESTOR?

A man is his own easiest dupe, for what he wishes to be true he generally believes to be true.

—DEMOSTHENES

I believe that there is a lack of clarity surrounding many of the terms we use to describe "trading." Traditionally, a trader was an order execution specialist—an individual whose job it was to fill the order flow coming in from his/her client base. The trader didn't exercise control or judgment over the buy/sell decision. Instead, the job was to quickly and efficiently execute the decision of others.

Wikipedia defines the word "speculation" as an activity that

involves the buying, holding, and selling of stocks, commodities, futures, currencies, collectibles, real estate, or any valuable thing to profit from fluctuations in its price as opposed to buying it for use or for income (via dividends, rent, etc).

In a world where direct electronic access to the world's markets is the norm, in most cases the role of the trader has been diminished or eliminated entirely. The words "trader" and "speculator" have now become interchangeable, but to be semantically correct, I am a speculator, and I would be willing to bet that 99.9 percent of those who ever open the pages of this book are speculators. The stock option, futures contract, or foreign currency pair that we choose to trade is simply a vehicle on which we practice our craft. The instrument matters little, its country of origin, currency denomination, or underlying asset may force us to adjust our trading plan slightly, but the instrument itself is simply an asset to be accumulated at one price, and distributed at another. To correctly define the role of an investor, we simply invert the definition of a speculator. Thus, an investor is

An individual who builds a position in stocks, commodities, futures, currencies, collectibles, real estate, or any valuable thing in an attempt to profit from the assets' capital appreciation or distributed income (via dividends, rent, etc).

When I, as a speculator purchase shares of IBM, I do so solely because I believe that the demand for these shares is about to rise. This increased demand should overwhelm the current level of supply, and as a result prices will rise. While I might analyze IBM's underlying business as a part of the decision to buy, I do so—solely—to determine if I believe it has a psychological ability to attract buyers. I am not interested in their business model, strategic vision, or long-term growth potential. I merely see an undervalued asset that I believe I can pick up "wholesale," mark up and sell at "retail" prices on a later date.

A great deal of money is lost by speculators who become investors inappropriately when a trade goes bad. They initiate the trade without a clear exit strategy in their trading plan (or more commonly lack a trading plan altogether), and then when the trade moves against them, they began researching the companies "long-term growth potential" in an effort to justify the position's continued existence. Not only do they invest their trading capital, but they invest a great deal of emotional capital as they try to justify their continued holding of this position.

Accumulation/Distribution Cycles

Whenever you feel there is confusion, go back to the roots of short-term price movement for clarity. Think in terms of a retail scenario.

Retail Scenario

The purchasing manager of a chain of clothing stores consults with the company's fashion advisers, and decides that colored jeans will be "in" this fall. The orders then are sent out into the manufacturing chain, and 50,000 pairs of red, yellow, and purple jeans are distributed to the company's stores in malls and shopping centers across the country. As the seasons change, and the back-to-school shopping surge matures, the red and purple products are selling very well. Upon taking inventory, the managers realize that the yellow jeans are not moving off the shelves. What do the business managers do next? They instruct the advertising department to begin featuring yellow jeans on the models in their next circular. The mannequins in the store windows all start wearing yellow jeans. They begin to promote the shade of yellow to the "movers and shakers" in the fashion industry. Soon, fashion designers on morning TV shows are promoting yellow as a "fresh new look," as they make over audience members.

These marketing and public relations attempts drive sales up slightly, but the public is just not interested in buying yellow jeans this season. So as the season winds down, the remaining inventory of unwanted yellow jeans goes on sale at a substantial discount. The store managers know that these low prices will change people's perceptions of the product and attract sales. Someone who would never pay $60 for a pair of yellow jeans, might pick up two pair and actually wear them if they only had to pay $18 for the product. The fads, manias, and ridiculous success/failure stories of the fashion industry offer close analogies to the world of speculation. The doughnut chain that enjoyed a $3 billion market cap for a short time is the polyester leisure suit of the stock market experience.

Financial Market Scenario

In this instance, a fund manager consults with the firm's analysts, and decides that the drug sector offers an attractive value at current prices. The decisions are made, the orders are submitted, and the fund is soon fully positioned long in a basket of 10 pharmaceutical stocks.

It turns out that the analyst's opinions were correct, the drug sector does indeed pick up over the next quarter as business begins to boom. Most of the stocks in the portfolio are showing a profit, but three are underperforming badly. FDA approval of a new drug has been delayed for one stock; one stock is working itself through a series of lawsuits, while another is experiencing poor sales due to a drug tampering scare. All of this negative publicity has dampened the public's interest in these issues. The fund begins to unwind these weak positions, selling into rallies and days of deep volume in an attempt to reduce slippage.

As the weeks pass, the rally in the pharmaceutical sector is picking up strength; the media begins to pick up on the sector's strength. Analysts are now being invited on the financial TV talk shows. Elsewhere in the financial press, bullish articles on the drug sector have begun to appear. Three months after the initial entries were taken, the fund's portfolio has been weeded down to the three best performers. Each of these positions has been trending well and is carrying a large paper profit. The fund manager begins to notice that the recent advances in these stocks have been unusually sluggish when compared to previous price action. The rally to date has been substantial, and there are large profits to be taken across the board. The advice to buy drug stocks has been everywhere, and has finally begun to filter down to the nonfinancial media. The talk around the office water cooler in average businesses has turned to the "killing" an associate made in PharmChem Industries. But as is usually the case, because the "crowd is always wrong," once the general public "knows" something about the market's trend—-the trend is nearing its end. The reality is that all of the "Smart Money" is already in these stocks. The traders and institutions with the money backing them at a level which can generate trend are not buyers anymore; they are now looking for excuses to take profits.

Trend lines begin to break, technical topping patterns form, and eventually we start to see the first lower high of the new downtrend on the daily chart. The funds begin to sell as these technical signals trigger the end of their trading opportunity. At first, these funds sell as opportunities present themselves intra day. As the selling intensifies, the funds see their profits slipping away from them and begin to hit the bid in an attempt to more aggressively unload their shares. With such a large open profit, they are willing to chase the stock down to a level where buyers are present in enough liquidity exists to fill their orders. The prices begin to plummet, and the bullish cycle in the sector has come to its end.

The Fear of Loss

Take a moment to look back over these two accumulation/distribution cycles. If you think about the realities of buying wholesale/selling retail, are these two stories really that different? Think in terms of the yellow pants. If the pants are deemed "ugly" by current standards, then why would anyone purchase a single pair? Two reasons spring to mind ... price and fashion. If the pants aren't selling, then the retailer can change the dynamic by lowering price or working to make yellow pants fashionable.

If you restate the question in the context of an individual equity, why would anyone who owns a stock sell it to us if it is about to go up in value? Why would anyone sell a stock that has delivered them a large paper profit? The answer to both of the scenarios is **fear of loss**. The owners will only sell their shares in a stock that is about to rally *if they don't see the rally coming!*

Quite the contrary, they foresee their stock's prices declining, and feel quite clever that they have found someone willing to take their risk off their hands! The speculator who takes their shares is operating from the opposite mindset. They feel clever that they have found some poor fool who is about to sell them shares that are about to dramatically rise in value! It is this never-ending difference of opinion that allows the financial marketplaces to experience the level of movement and liquidity needed for successful speculation.

Reasons to Sell

As a trader/speculator, there are three basic forms that selling may take:

1. selling because the trend is changing, and profitable positions are being unwound,

2. selling because resistance levels are being challenged and positions are being lightened or exited,
3. and selling because a chart pattern or technical setup has failed and stop-loss orders are being triggered in the marketplace.

A stock experiencing the first form of selling should be traded with a short bias, as it is likely that sellers will control the trend in the near future. A stock experiencing the second form of selling should be treated with a long bias, with a focus on buying continuation patterns and implementing other low risk trend trading tactics. A stock experiencing the third form of selling can be "gamed" in the smaller time frames as either a profitable scalp trade, or a way to "fade" for a more advantageous entry.

For a number of years I have been actively writing, analyzing, and presenting my trading ideas in public. This public presence has brought me into contact with hundreds of traders at seminars and speaking engagements around the world. By definition, a consistently profitable trader is unlikely to take the time to attend a seminar. Therefore, most of the traders I work with are struggling and frustrated with their speculative returns. They listen carefully as I present my strategies and ideas, but are often quite shocked at how simple my trading plans are. They often believe I am holding out some "super secret" pattern or indicator that would magically erase all of their problems!

Trader's Learning Curve

There seems to be a very consistent learning curve that successful traders go through as they gain skills and build a profitable trading strategy. It sometimes amazes me how similarly traders share experiences—both good and bad—as they develop their trading skills.

Mystification Stage

We all begin our trading careers in what I term the "mystification" stage. We don't yet fully understand how supply and demand dictate price movement, and are unaware of the quite comprehensive body of work surrounding the analysis of market structure and technical price action. The price charts we see on television or on the World Wide Web are little more than meaningless squiggles of color. The idea that anyone could look into this seemingly random data and correctly divine the future seems improbable, if not quite a mystical concept. Slowly but surely, the beginning trader builds his/her knowledge base, using books, courses, and seminars—all resources available to the modern speculator. As her chart reading ability expands, she begins to see squiggles dissolve into price patterns and setups on her charts.

"Hot Pot" Phase

Our beginning trader now enters the "hot pot" phase. He scans the markets and notices that one particular price pattern from his books seems to be producing consistent profits. Excited at the prospect of beginning to actually trade, he zeros in on this one setup and begins paper trading to see if "he can make money." Typically, when there is no actual capital at risk, the beginner will forget the stopped trades and remember vividly the setups that reach their profit objectives! This selective memory builds a false sense of security and pressure to not "miss out" on any more profits. The trader's excitement grows and grows until finally he can't stand it: *"Every paper trade I made last week would have produced a profit. This is it! I'm taking the next setup for real!"*

He steps up and finally puts real capital at risk. Ka-Bam! The trade triggers, then turns on a dime and races back down to trigger his stop-loss levels. Chastised by this loss, the beginning trader scratches his head and goes back to paper trading. Sure enough, as soon as he begins paper trading again, the pattern starts producing profits immediately. This cycle repeats as he waits to see the "perfect patterns," marshals his bravery, and takes the next trade for real.

By now you should be able to identify this as a classic payout/payback cycle mismanagement error. Our beginning trader will only be likely to see perfect patterns during the winning streak of a payout cycle. Then, as he gathers his courage to trade, the market flips back into a more chaotic payback environment and his real money trade will have a high probability to produce nothing more then failure and loss.

This cycle of observed pleasure and experienced pain heightens emotionality and frustration levels. The research and testing phase is still challenging and fun for our hot pot trader, but trading itself becomes a negative experience; one to be feared and possibly avoided. It is much the same situation as a child who touches a hot pot on the stove and burns a finger. After getting burned once or twice, he becomes afraid of the pot, not understanding that it is the *flame beneath the pot* that makes it harmful.

Cynical Phase

It is horribly frustrating to have studied so hard, and to have your efforts produce nothing but universal failure. Even worse, it seems that the strategies and setups you are tracking seem to fail only when you take them! This experience tends to breed a level of disgust and cynicism towards trading that I term the "cynical skepticism" stage. This is the stage where the majority of traders gets stuck and washes out of the trading game.

They leave the markets feeling betrayed and convinced that the books, seminars, and course materials they tried to learn from must have all been lies! All of these inputs claimed that their ideas would produce a profitable outcome, yet every time the cynical skeptic took such trades they turned into losing propositions! These losses hurt all the more because there were so many observed or paper traded setups that would have produced enormous gains.

One of the most painful experiences for any person is to fail when competency and success seem simple. This experience of failure breeds anger, frustration, and embarrassment, which is diverted by the cynical skeptic into defensive anger—anger at the evil market makers who manipulated the market in order to trigger stops, and anger at the instructors who showed them the strategies that ended up causing so much emotional pain. "Those people *must* be snake oil salesman" because if they were all frauds and charlatans, the cynical skeptic's trading failures would be explained away.

This blame game might be satisfying to your ego in the very short term, but to become just another whiny loser guarantees that you will never achieve your goal of success as a speculator. If you believe that there is always a grand external conspiracy working against you, there is no reason for you to spend time looking inward in an attempt to analyze why you failed. While many people live their lives with an excuse driven mindset outside the markets, to do so as a trader guarantees your demise.

Squiggle Trading Stage

Those traders with the emotional maturity to move beyond the cynical skepticism stage often find themselves mired in what I call the morass of "squiggle trading." They feel certain that there is some secret weapon, some system, strategy, or indicator out there that will help them avoid the losing trades that caused them such consternation and emotional pain. They justify their previous losses as being due to simple ignorance. They are convinced that all they need to do is find **"IT"** and all their goals and dreams will be achieved. They begin an obsessive love affair with the markets, often to the exclusion of social life, love life, and work life. They buy every book, and purchase every course in the hopes that these materials will contain the Holy Grail they seek. In doing so, they set themselves up for failure, as they try desperately to buy their success as a trader. We know this to be a natural human tendency, as proven by the weekend golfer who puts off going to the practice range, but who is willing to spend $600 on a new driver which will do little more than enable him to put the ball 10 yards further into the woods! The patterns, indicators, and strategies the squiggle trader purchases may all have edge and worth, but they are not enough, by themselves, to create profitability.

The squiggle trader further confounds the learning curve by stacking indicator after indicator and strategy after strategy onto the same chart. While each trading tool may have strong predictive abilities on its own, too many inputs guarantee underperformance as paralysis by over analysis sets in. There are just too many different ways to trade, too many indicators, and too many time frames available to the squiggle trader. It is a virtual certainty, at some point every day these strategies will all flash conflicting buy and sell signals.

With so many conflicting inputs to analyze, the squiggle trader becomes a deer in the headlights and fails to make *any* decisions whatsoever! Or what is worse, once a position has been initiated, the squiggle trader will seek out only those trading indicators/strategies that agree with the current trade. This selective analysis process ruins any chance at objectivity or consistent profitability.

Trade justification is one of the hallmarks of scared or ignorant money. Lacking a clear understanding or acceptance of risk, the squiggle trader essentially expends time and effort looking for sources that agree with them. This is a highly destructive trading behavior for two reasons: First, it transfers all responsibility for the success or failure of your position to an outside source and second, it promotes emotional whipsaws that will shake you out of what would've been profitable trades. When your stochastic says sell, and your CCI says buy, which indicator are you supposed to listen to? Faced with such an uncertain scenario, many squiggle traders will simply abandon what could have been a profitable trade in order to mitigate their psychological unease.

As difficult as the squiggle trader phase can be, I believe it is an extremely important step in any trader's development. I certainly was an extraordinarily confused squiggle trader for much of my second year as a full-time trader. But in spite of its frustrations, this phase of development taught me a great deal about what other traders are doing, and which techniques, tactics, and indicators are most popular with the trading/investing public. This information was invaluable to me later on as I began to develop my theories about payout/payback cycles and liquidity pools as magnets for price. Because I had been the "greater fool" so many times, I knew what constituencies were likely to be active in any given market, and more importantly how an unsophisticated trader is likely to react to stimuli. I think you must spend some time trapped in a squiggle trader phase in order to be an effective fade, squeeze, or trap trader later on in your career.

The squiggle trader phase can be a bit of emotional quicksand from which many traders never break free. They will spend the rest of their trading career looking for their Holy Grail, and while some may achieve periods of consistent profitability as they search, they will never realize their full potential as speculators.

Inwardly Bound Phase

For those who pass beyond the squiggle trader phase, a whole new world of profitability awaits. I strongly believe it takes some catalyst in the form of a mentor or powerful learning experience to break one free from the morass of squiggle trading. Because having "seen the light," you realize that all of the answers you seek come from within, and the markets begin to unfold before you like a rare and precious flower. Instead of battlefields you see playgrounds. Instead of squeezes, failures, and pain you see predictability, opportunity, and large risk-to-reward ratios!

You become comfortable with your competency as a trader. You have confidence in your analysis skills and begin to specialize in just a few edges as you hone in on the markets and strategies which offer you your greatest profitability. Much of your growth and development during this phase will be personal, and fairly profound. I also believe it is worthwhile to study the concepts of Zen, as I find them to be very much in alignment with the emotional mindset of the long time successful trader.

Once you pass through the squiggle trader phase, you enter a final phase I call the "inwardly bound" stage. This is an exciting time for any trader. You begin to realize that the true Holy Grails of trading are: risk management, the power of your trading plan, and an effective payout/payback cycle management strategy. As an inwardly bound trader, you understand that **YOU** have total control over the market risk you assume, and perhaps for the first time in your trading career, are taking total responsibility for your trades. Your trading plan has been developed with thought and care, and you don't deviate from those plans. You always honor your stops, and manage your market risk with a non-emotional, truly objective frame of mind (the majority of the time). The craving to impulsively place or scratch trades has been reduced or eliminated.

Your profitability increases now through flashes of insight which increase your existing strategy's edge. You are more and more comfortable taking larger market risks and your average yearly income has exploded as a result. The most interesting byproduct of this time in your trading career is the development of your intuitive side as a trader. You will not be able to effectively explain at times why you have a certain opinion about market direction, but you will "know" that something big is about to happen. These intuitive trades will be infrequent, but can be extraordinarily profitable as they often correctly predict an enormous shock event about to occur in the marketplace.

Much like remembering in a flash the face of someone you haven't spoken with in years, you must open yourself to the possibility that your subconscious can often remember and replay situations your conscious mind forgets. Experiment with these trades at first, but be ready to increase your size as trust in your gut builds.

Ironically, just such a scenario is unfolding as I put this chapter down on paper. The equity markets worldwide have had an exceptional run, and euphoric conditions have been showing themselves across many sectors. I have been calling for a top now for several weeks, but have been stymied as new highs are seen week after week. None of the reversal patterns that are in my trading plans have been seen, so I have not had a valid trigger upon which to begin building a short position. Last

Wednesday, as I scanned the markets after the close for opportunity, my skin started to crawl as my gut screamed GET SHORT NOW! I have learned over time that these intuitive opinions are more often accurate, so I shorted the Dow Industrials using a futures instrument the next morning as soon as I got up. The market fell 90 points that session, and as I write this it sure looks like there will be more downside coming once trading opens again next week. Only time will tell how powerful an entry my intuition gave me, but as it stands I am short with approximately 3.2 to 1 in open profits and the chance for more profits if this short term top turns out to be something more significant. Epilogue: The market fell off violently after this entry was taken, and the "gut" based position yielded more then 350 points in profit.

Master Phase

The final stage of trader development is mastery. For the master trader, trading becomes second nature. Your own unique trading style is such a part of who you are, that it doesn't take conscious effort anymore to analyze the market and follow your trading plan once opportunity has been identified.

To use a sports term, you have achieved a level of *unconscious competence* as a speculator. Once you have reached a level of unconscious competence you will find that you can still trade with profitable effectiveness through times of stress or distraction that would have provoked gross trading errors in the past. You can get up in the middle of the night to use the bathroom, peek at the foreign exchange markets, and—groggy as you may be—will put on what turns out to be an extremely profitable position before heading back to bed. You can trade without errors in front of an audience, while talking on the phone, or after a long night on the town.

I have experienced my own trial by fire in this way as a member of my family has been battling cancer for the past five years. Trading throughout this often difficult time has tested my own unconscious competence, and my lack of emotionally based trading errors, in spite of these market external worries and stresses, remains my proudest accomplishment as a trader. Once you reach this level in your trading career, the act of trading itself becomes a "thoughtless" endeavor. Developing your trade plan and researching and developing new edges as the market environment shifts, become your primary focus. You begin to view the trade plan development process, much as a professional athlete views a scrimmage. This is where you focus effort—planning for and anticipating all outcomes—so that the killer instinct is there to make the big play without hesitation when the market offers it.

Believe me when I tell you that I know each step of the learning curve intimately. I certainly worked my way through each and every one of the phases outlined above. Every one of the theories, ideas, strategies, and beliefs about trader development that I have and talk about, come from personal experience. During my path from zero to hero, I have experienced levels of intense emotional pain, frustration, dejection, and depression that were only matched by the serious life-threatening illness of a parent.

From these terrible lows, I have also experienced highs of the same intensity. This manic-depressive existence was not a healthy one, and certainly wasn't conducive to consistent profitability. Learning to manage these cycles was a critical hurdle for me if I wanted to survive my learning curve. This is why so many traders burn out and quit this business before they ever have a chance to achieve their potential. You must learn to accept the manic depressive cyclicality of trading for a living, and separate its crazy extremes from your own day-to-day emotional existence.

I stumbled most of the way through the learning curve by myself, then was lucky enough early on to find several close friends in the business. As we compared our experiences, I soon became aware that many of my highs and lows were not unique in the least. These friends had gone through, or were going through the same challenges and frustrations. As I matured as a trader, I came to treasure the manic craziness of this business. After all, if this were a simple endeavor, everyone would be enjoying the freedom and strong profitability the markets can offer. (And the amount of money available to us as traders would be very small!) The reason the potential for such incredible income exists for traders is *because* this is such a difficult business to be in! Don't give up!

CHAPTER 7

WHY MARKETS MOVE

Prices, like everything else, move along the line of least resistance. They will do whatever comes easiest, therefore they will go up if there is less resistance to an advance than a decline; and vice versa.

—JESSE LIVERMORE

A financial market, whether it is the virtual world of the CME E-Minis, or the very physical exchanges of the CBOT and NYSE is, at its core, an endless auction. Prices go up because supplies are limited. Buyers driven by their belief in future price increases bid up the price in order to fill their bullish positions. Prices go down because supply is overabundant, and buyers feel that if they exercise a little patience, they will likely be offered a chance to buy later on at a deep discount. A successful speculator, no matter what his strategy, is a treasure hunter, looking for those golden moments in time when the market's endless auction *mis*-prices an asset.

This process is often driven by a lack of focus by the investing public. Consider the following example. If a famous car collector dies, and his estate is put up for auction, car collectors and automobile enthusiasts from around the world will gather to bid on the items from his collection. His rarest and most prized possessions will likely demand a powerful

premium as the world's top car collectors compete for owner-
ship of these rare specimens. The focus of the auction is automobiles, and the supply of automobiles is not enough to satisfy
the demand from the car collectors on hand. Because all the
marketing surrounding this event was focused on automobiles,
it is unlikely that anyone traveled to bid on the furnishings
from his formal dining room. Despite the fact that these
wonderful antiques were worth a great deal of money, they
sold for pennies on the dollar. At this auction, there was a great
deal of supply in terms of furniture, but little demand. This
theoretical scenario highlights the contrary nature of speculation. If you're passionate interest is in owning a 1935 Auburn
"Boat Tail" Speedster, your focus is on the car, and while you
hope you can acquire this specimen for your collection at a
reasonable price, the price itself is a secondary issue.

Speculate for Profit

If you are a speculator however, whose interest in the auction
is solely profit oriented, you should ignore the cars entirely and
buy every stick of furniture that is being sold at a discount. The
furniture is your inventory. It can be accumulated cheaply, then
marked up and sold at fair value or for a slight premium. In the
stock market, just like in this auto action, the "bargains" will
exist outside the current "fashion." If drug stocks are in vogue,
with coverage in the financial media, then perhaps the telecom-
munications sector has been overlooked and is offering an
elegant entry. If gold stocks are "hot," then perhaps the finan-
cials are beaten down and stocks are selling at attractive prices.

The world's financial markets are a central clearing house
for opinion, and economic prognostication. There is always
a crowd consensus about where prices are headed, and why
they will be moving in that direction. There are few absolute

truths in the speculative world other than the mathematics of accuracy and risk-to-reward ratios and one of them is:

The crowd is always wrong, the market will always move AGAINST the directional opinion of current consensus.

The sooner you internalize this concept as absolute truth, the sooner you'll change your thinking from that of the majority (who usually lose) to the minority (who usually win.) By truly understanding why markets move, you'll be in a position to more clearly identify when and where "the crowd" has positioned themselves. If you believe that the crowd is always wrong, and the market is always going to move against the directional opinion of current consensus, then to create a profitable trading strategy, all one has to do is figure out how the crowd is positioned, and bet against them!

Identify Crowd Directional Opinions

Before we try to understand how best to identify the crowd's directional opinions, we need to delve into a few of the realities of short-term price movement. Over the "long term," equity prices will be determined by the fundamental value and success or failure of the underlying business operations. However, in my opinion a true long term investor exposes himself to an unacceptable level of account volatility for the amount of profits it would be reasonable to expect. Simply put, the risk-to-reward ratios of the long term investor (while profitable), are grossly inferior to those available to even the most inexperienced speculator.

Take the very typical investment experience from an investor holding stock in Boeing (see Figure 7.1) If the investment was established in the late 1990s, it is likely that the investor would have built a position with an average price near $45–$50

Monthly   BA-BOEING CO
1996 1997 1998 1999 2000 2001 2002 2003 2004 2005 2006 2007

Figure 7.1

per share. The fundamental basis for this investment could have been based on the age of the world's commercial airframes, the opinion that new models would be a great success and greatly increase Boeing's earnings. But really, the reasoning does not matter. It is the risk assumed by the investor that I want you to focus on. Remember that the conventional wisdom, the crowd mentality is that speculation is a wild gamble while investing for the "long haul" is the only safe bet.

Granted, this investment is up approximately 100 percent over the course of ten years so technically it has been a great pick. However, look at all the dead money years and violent sell offs the investor had to endure in order to participate in Boeing's recent rally. At one point, the investment would have been down a little more then 50 percent. Think of the pain and frustration that a 50 percent draw down would provoke, especially after nearly 8 years of nonperformance. Just think how many investor's capitulated during that time and thus totally missed out on the subsequent rally!

If taken in absolute terms, the investment can be said to have generated a 2 to 1 risk-to-reward ratio. (A 50 percent draw down that resulted eventually in a 100 percent gain.) However, I would argue strongly that the risk of a long term investor is essentially 80–90 percent of capital invested. If they follow the buy and hold mentality with strict discipline, then there will be investments that dwindle away 80–90 percent of the capital invested. Very few will actually go bankrupt, so I put the actual assumed risk to the average investor in the 80–90 percent zone. With this more realistic assessment of reality based risk, the Boeing trade has really only delivered a little more then a 1 to 1 risk-to-reward ratio.

If you have index funds, or any broadly diversified mutual fund in your portfolio, chances are high that it includes exposure to the stock of Microsoft. (See Figure 7.2)

If the investment was established in the late 1990s, you are likely showing a small profit, but any positions taken during 1999 or 2000 are seriously underwater. Not only that, but this

Figure 7.2

stock has been dead money for the past seven years. It has tied up the capital of the long term investor without offering any compensation for the time wasted, or the risk that it could break support near $20 per share and trade down to the $10 area. If I was testing a new trading idea to determine its edge, and saw this kind of non performance and poor risk-to-reward ratio, I would dump it like a hot potato and move on to the next idea! It is staggering to me how much money investors lose or worse leave on the table due to basic ignorance about the markets and where it gives up its profits.

As dismissive as I feel about buy and hold investing as a strategy, I have nothing against long holding periods *if they are managed using all the principles of risk management that I believe in!* Following is a trade that I personally held that adhered to these principles.

The stock was from the energy sector, and I felt that the sector as a whole was turning its trend from bear to bull. As you can see from the monthly chart in Figure 7.3, CMS Energy

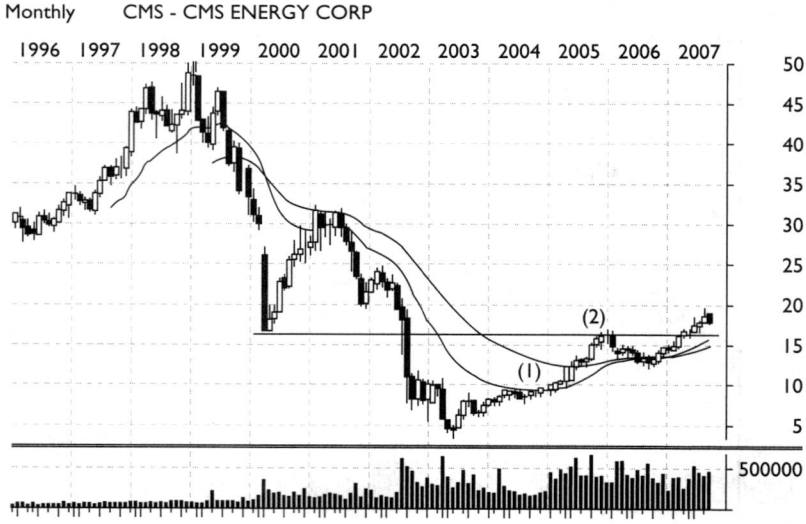

Figure 7.3

Corp. had been trading within the context of a severe down-trend ever since its top in late 1998. Price had done nothing but fall with the exception of one bear market correction in 2000. After capitulating near $5 per share, CMS rallied up to test areas of round number resistance near $10 per share. Instead of rolling over at resistance, the stock began to fight for its life. This was the first real gumption the stock had shown in many years, and it was valid to enter as its weekly price formation was one of the price patterns that I use as a buy signal (1). I was able to put on the position with a very small amount of risk, and therefore due to my position sizing strategy had a fairly large position size. As the chart shows, CMS did change its trend, and rallied smoothly up to test an area of chart resist-ance just above the $15 per share level (2). This trade was open for about 13 months, and paid me a risk-to-reward ratio of more then 20 to 1.

I am sure the trade would have been seen as an investment by many market participants. I suspected that there was some fairly strong fundamental value in the stock when I took my initial entry, but it is important to note that the stock was not purchased for its "cheapness," but rather for its reward poten-tial. I felt that if CMS could change its trend, it would have a ton of room in which to rally as it moved up to test chart resist-ance. The potential reward of this move would more then off-set any possible risk of failure. So even if you love a particular company, and are certain that purchasing its shares would be a fine long-term investment, always utilize the tools and tactics of the active trader to properly position size and set protective stop-loss orders for each of your long time holdings. The draw downs you avoid, and the increased reward you capture will compound into very serious money by the time you are ready to retire.

Within the context of the deep–time-frame trends of funda-mental valuation, markets cycle endlessly between overbought

Insider's Advice Never forget that speculation is a zero sum game, one in which money flows out of the pockets of those less experienced, less informed, less aggressive market participants into the bank accounts of those speculators who along with discipline and a trading plan have the experience, information, and aggressiveness the unprofitable speculator lacks.

and oversold levels relative to the "mean." It is these extremes of fear and greed that offer the disciplined speculator a consistent source of income in all market environments. Nowhere are these moments of greed and fear more violent or emotionally based than in the intraday time frames.

Whereas a position trader, operating off of a daily and weekly chart might be making management decisions every seven to 10 days, the intraday trader goes through this decision-making cycle every seven to 10 minutes! The acceleration and time pressures of the intraday markets creates a pressure cooker in which even experienced traders tend to commit the most basic rookie errors. Because of this tendency, and the immediacy of feedback on one's directional opinion, the intraday markets are a wonderful vehicle to use for training, strategy development, and experience building. The skill set that you build as a day trader makes some of the slower (and in my experience, more profitable) trading styles seem like a walk in the park by comparison.

Price Charts

The basic tool for speculative analysis is the price/time chart. From the freely available Web sites to the finest in professional real time data packages, a price chart is the primary trade generation tool for today's professional speculator. The most

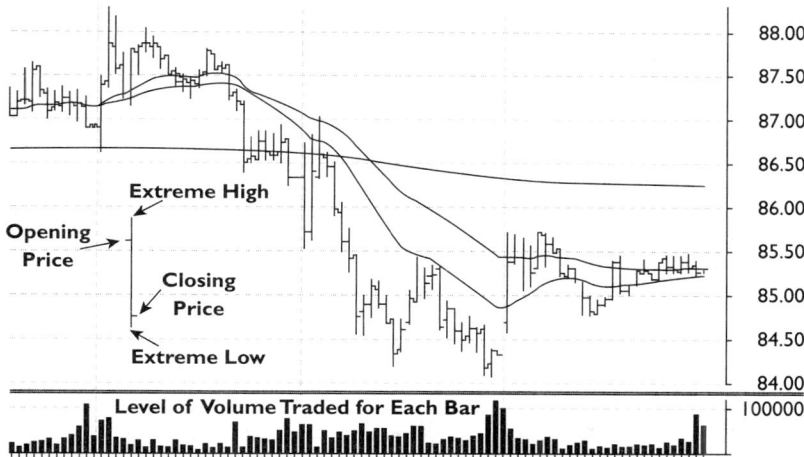

Figure 7.4 Example of a bar chart

common chart type you will see on most trading desks is the simple bar chart (see Figure 7.4).

Each bar represents the price action a market experienced during a predefined period of time. A weekly bar chart draws a new bar for each week's worth of data; a daily bar chart draws a bar which contains the price action from each trading day. Intraday bar charts are designated by their time period measured in minutes. Five minute, fifteen minutes, and hourly bars are the most common time frames utilized by most intra day traders. Each "bar" consists of a vertical line which desig-nates the extreme high and low price experienced during the charting period. A small horizontal tick on the left side of the line is drawn to indicate the opening price, while a tick on the right side of the bar designates the closing price. The histogram at the bottom of the chart denotes the number of shares or contracts traded within the bars time period.

While bar charts are most common, I prefer to use the Japanese method of "candlestick" charting to view market data (see Figure 7.5). A candlestick chart is simply a bar chart with

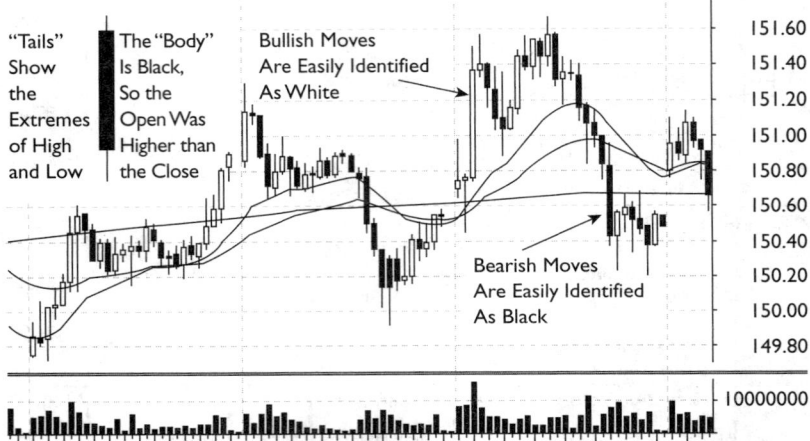

Figure 7.5 Example of a candlestick chart

a box drawn around the opening and closing levels for each period. This box or "body" is then filled in white or green for a candle that increases in value—opens low and closes high; red or black for a candle that decreases in value—opens high, then closes low. Any extremes in price that occur outside the candles' body are shown as vertical lines or "tails." These color-coded candlesticks, with their bodies and tails, create recognizable price patterns that become icons for reversal and price rejection. With a little practice, you will be able to instantly identify the areas on a price chart where support or resistance manifested itself. This speed of analysis will add to your agility and edge as a trader.

There is a complicated discipline of trading that is based entirely on candlestick specific price patterns (see Figure 7.6). While a "Dark Cloud Cover," or "Hanging Man" can indeed represent a trend reversal, in my experience these patterns are not robust enough to provide a sustainable edge on their own. I use candlestick charts for two simple reasons. First, a candlestick chart makes momentum driven trend moves extremely easy to identify. These sustained bullish or bearish drives show

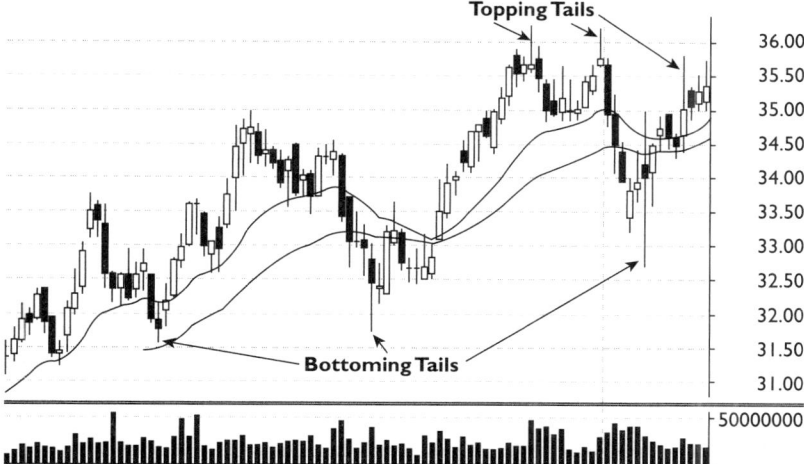

Figure 7.6 Candlestick chart with topping tails and bottoming tails

up plain and clear as black or white "price thrusts." Second and most important, the tails on a candlestick chart allow you to tell in an instant where the market has rejected a price test. If the market rallies into an area of resistance (an area where there are more sellers than buyers), then the market will likely reverse to the downside, leaving a "topping tail" on its candlestick chart. Inversely, when a market reaches down to test an area of support, the price will often reverse and form a "bottoming tail" that can be easily identified on a candlestick style chart. Since markets tend to trend up and down in waves, when a topping tail is seen after an extended move to the upside, it often reveals that a tradable reversal is occurring. The relationship between the size of the tail and the candle's body can also act as an indicator to the power and violence of the reversal.

For the professional speculator, any predictable movement in the markets offers a chance for profit. Money can be made through short sales during a market decline, or more traditionally on the long side as a market rallies. The professional

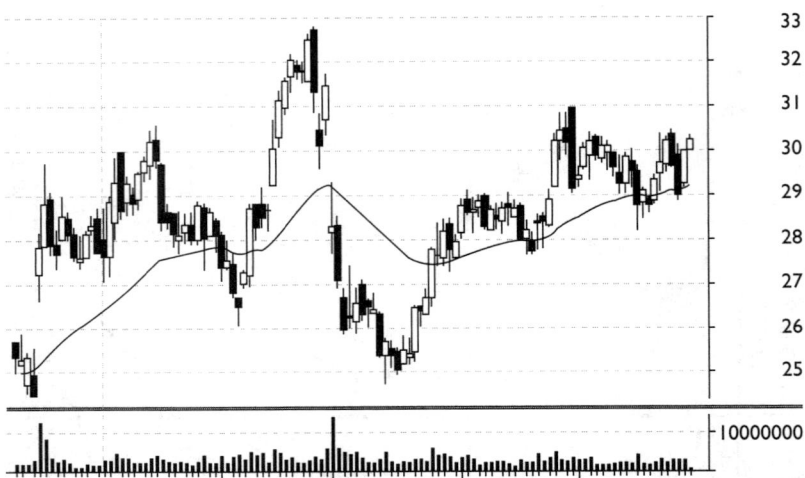

Figure 7.7

speculator doesn't care where the market goes, as long as it offers enough actionable information to get on board and participate in the movement! The amateur looks at Figure 7.7, and sees little of interest or use. The stock began the year at one price, and looks as if it will end the year without any significant gain or loss.

The professional looks at this same stock, and sees many potentially profitable swings in price. There were tests of support and resistance, topping and bottoming tails, reversal patterns, and plenty of actionable information available to trade with over the course of a year. When I look at Figure 7.8, I see the following price patterns that would have indicated entry into this stock.

1. a short signal as a "peek" reversal pattern forms
2. a pullback to gap
3. a bearish engulfing bar
4. a rally to moving average resistance coupled with a large topping tail

Figure 7.8

5. a pullback to areas of moving average support
6. another pullback to moving average support

Where the amateur sees nothing, the more informed speculator sees any number of opportunities to make money. While
the amateur looks for fast movement and big swings, the experienced trader knows that predictability is not the size of the
movement, but the ability to enter with the smallest stop size in
a lower volatility stock that will deliver the risk-to-reward ratios
needed to capture superior profits. Even a boring baser like the
example above can produce beautifully, if traded properly.

CHAPTER 8

THE MAJORITY IS *ALWAYS* WRONG

*Truth always rests with the minority, and the minority is
always stronger than the majority, because the minority is
generally formed by those who really have an opinion, while
the strength of a majority is illusory, formed by the gangs who
have no opinion—and who, therefore, in the next instant
(when it is evident that the minority is the stronger) assume
its opinion—while Truth again reverts to a new minority.*

—SØREN KIERKEGAARD

I f we truly believe that the crowd is always wrong, and that
the market will always move against the directional opinion
of current consensus, then our first order of business is to
determine the following:

1. Who is the crowd? Which constituencies are actively
   trading in the marketplace?
2. Which trading strategies is the crowd employing?
3. Where will the crowd's psychological trigger points and
   stop-loss levels likely be set?

20-period Exponential Moving Average

One of the most commonly taught and understood trend continuation patterns is the pullback to the support level offered by a 20-period Exponential Moving Average (EMA). The 20-period EMA is an arbitrary level, but has great relevance in the modern financial marketplace *simply because the majority of traders believe that it does!*

When technical analysis and other classic pattern recognition systems were developed, the process of charting was a labor-intensive endeavor implemented manually with pen and paper. Few at the time understood the concepts, and fewer were even willing to do the work it took to implement these strategies. Fast forward to the new millennium, and now even the beginning trader can identify flags, pendants, cup and handle breakouts, double tops, and double bottoms.

The financial press and the advent of the Internet have made this technical knowledge available to every trader worldwide. As a result, when tested, the 20-period EMA often provokes a surge in order flow because the majority of traders watching the market have trading strategies built around this purely technical level. When the 20 EMA is tested, it is guaranteed there will be a surge of buy orders entering the market! The educational programs and articles available to the public teach that a pullback to the 20-period EMA is the "holy grail buy signal." Therefore, the bullish order flow triggered by the 20-period EMA is entering the market for purely technical reasons. Since this is the case, these pullback setups offer the savvy speculator a chance to observe how the market reacts to surge in bullish order flow. If the market reverses, and gives every indication that support is manifesting itself, then an entry can be taken on the assumption that the trend is about to resume.

Another common crowd trigger point is seen when the market breaks out to a new high or low. There are more strategies built around breakouts than you can shake a stick at, and the speculative focus that surrounds these break points can offer the knowledgeable speculator any number of edge filled strategies to exploit. Since you can count on a ton of buy signals bringing bullish order flow into the market any time a stock breaks out, the informed speculator can sit back and take entry based on how the market reacts to the crowd's order flow. Sometimes it is best to align your position with the herd, but fading the crowd is another strategy that can offer rich rewards to the chart reader who waits to see how the market will react to the increase in order activity.

This observational and reactionary trading style is what I use for my personal trading accounts. By using technically driven order flow not as a predictive event, but as a *stimulative one*, I "chart read" myself into long or short positions as the market trends shift. By interpreting the market's reaction to a surge in order flow, I use the crowd's actions to provoke the market into revealing its true line of least resistance.

Thousands of pages have been written on the subject of technical analysis and charting financial markets, so I will not try to cover the subject in depth here. Instead, I hope to communicate my philosophy for technical trading. This is a universal concept, and can be applicable to whatever technical analysis method you are comfortable with. It will be an effective way to increase your edge if you are using indicators or oscillators, Fibonacci or other market geometry strategies, as well as most pattern recognition models. Although many of these tactics can yield an edge, I have found that the simplest principles are the most powerful, profitable, and repeatable both for myself and my clients. Don't let yourself get seduced by the "cuteness" of any given analysis style. It is extremely likely that there is a

Figure 8.1

simple strategy staring you in the face that will offer a great deal more edge with a far less complicated set of entry and exit rules.

In Figure 8.1, we see a stock that is trading within the context of an established uptrend. Driven by an abundance of demand, the stock rallies until short-term demand is satisfied, then rolls over and begins to sell off as each wave of profit taking hits the market. Each time the 20-period EMA is tested [(1),(2),(3)], the bulls return to the market, and the uptrend resumes. The advance/decline cycle has just started another correction phase, and is pulling back to test 20-period EMA support yet again. Because the stock is in an uptrend, we begin our analysis process with bullish bias. We will watch how the stock trades in the next session, and hope to initiate a long entry if the buy orders triggered by the 20-period EMA provoke a "correct reaction."

Now take a look at our potential trade as the market nears the close the following day. As you can see from Figure 8.2, the increase in bullish order flow provoked by the 20-period EMA

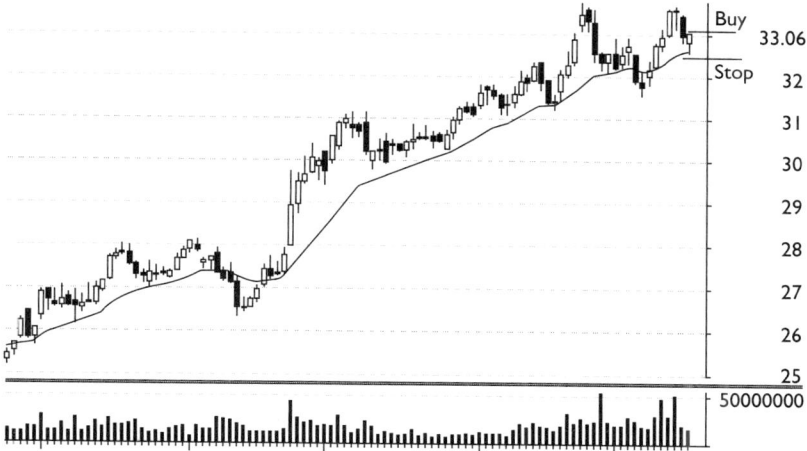

Figure 8.2

quickly overwhelmed demand and formed a reversal in the stock. A traditional setup would be to buy the stock if it breaks above the highs of that reversal bar with protective stop-loss orders set just under the bar's lows. Since this traditional entry/stop-loss pairing is so widely understood, these points are where the crowd are likely to cluster their orders.

This tendency creates "liquidity pools" just above the reversal bars extreme high and low. Markets tend to seek out areas of high liquidity, so the probability is extremely high that price will reach out to the high of the bar tomorrow in order to soak up its liquidity pool. Once the liquidity pool of buy orders has been satisfied, the market will begin moving along the line of least resistance to the most easily available liquidity pool. In most pullback patterns, the most accessible liquidity pool lies just above the breakout point to a new high. This is why more often than not I target a retest of the previous high as my profit objective when trading pullbacks to support.

As I worked through my personal learning curve as a trader, I came to believe strongly in the statement that the crowd was always wrong. Often, when I deconstructed my losing trades, I would realize that the trade failed because I had taken my position in alignment with the crowd's directional opinion. Never one to adopt a belief on faith alone, I tried to figure out *why* the market always moved against the directional opinion of current consensus. After all, if demand overcomes supply, then prices will rise. If the crowd was buying due to a technical setup, then why would the market often reverse in what felt like a personally assaultive, malignant manner?

There are times as a trader when you are convinced that the market hates your guts, and is personally persecuting you every time you initiate a trade. I have literally had clients in my consulting practice who asked me if it was possible that their broker was leaking information about their positions to the market makers. The market makers are often treated like some kind of superstitious boogeymen, who are always trading "against you." These feelings of frustration and paranoia are common to traders because they are consistently taking positions with the crowd! Remember:

> *The crowd is always wrong, the market will always move AGAINST the directional opinion of current consensus.*

Therefore, these frustrated traders lose, not due to some grand conspiracy against them, but because of the simple fact that markets seek liquidity in the smaller time frames. This liquidity pool theory is something I developed many years ago, and have really never seen discussed in a public area before. I believe it is one of the most important realizations of my trading career. I hope by describing *why* the market always seems to trade against you, you will be able to move away from your majority aligned trading behavior, and begin profiting as a new constituent of the minority.

Figure 8.3

By definition, traders don't seek out my help unless they are frustrated and in pain due to losses or underperformance in their trading programs. As part of the initial interview, I ask to look at some of their recent trades. Figure 8.3 shows a classic pullback trade that blew up in everybody's face. To begin with, we see a market trading within the context of a strong uptrend. Higher highs and higher lows are printed, and each test of support results in reversal and trend continuation. The last pullback was stable and clean. It tested areas of support and printed a clear reversal candlestick (1). The price then rallied to break above that reversal candlestick's high, and then waffled for several bars. It then gathered its strength and looked like it would follow through to its profit objectives. Just as soon as everything seemed copacetic, price reversed, and the bottom dropped out of the market (2). You can see the "bloom" in volume as the market's decline triggered protective stop-loss orders below the reversal bar's low (3).

Emotionally, the pullback traders went on a roller coaster ride from anticipation to confirmation to euphoric exultation to consternation to depressive frustration. It is very understandable that the pullback trader caught in this pattern failure would feel personally targeted by the market. But as usual when dealing with the markets, emotions lie. Here is what actually happened on a fundamental level step by step.

The market first tested an area of technical support. Traders are taught to initiate positions against support levels, so this test brought a surge of demand to the market. The technically triggered buy orders overcame the market's current level of supply, and prices began to rise (see Figure 8.4). This reversal in the supply/demand balance was graphically represented as a reversal candlestick (1).

This reversal candlestick acted as another technical buy signal to the candlestick trading community, and this trigger brought additional demand to the market. The waves of demand driven by these different buy signals caused the market to begin oscillating as demand began to fight to overcome supply. Each time it rallied, *more* technical trading strategies triggered their buy signals as moving averages crossed over,

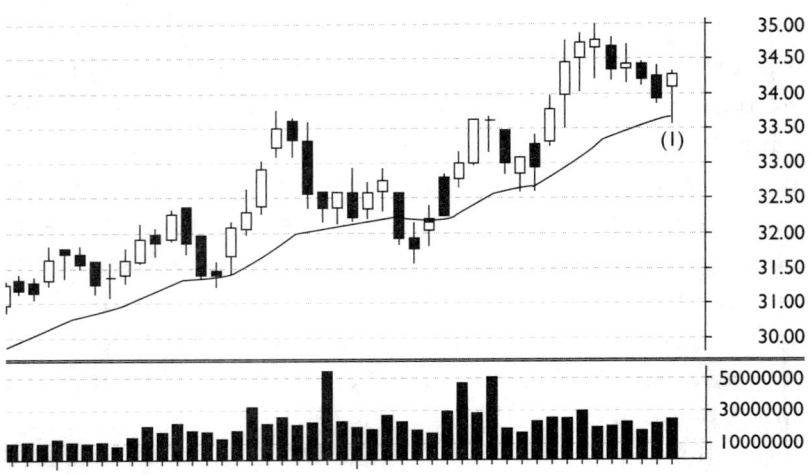

Figure 8.4

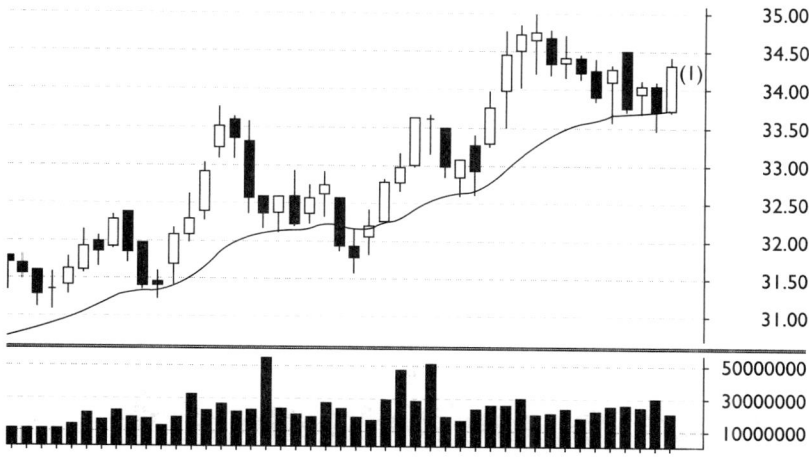

Figure 8.5

stochastics, and CCI gave their entry triggers, and reversal candlesticks in deeper time frames began to form (see Figure 8.5). After four days of struggle, the bears gave up the fight, and the stock printed a solid bullish (white) trend bar (1).

After all the technical setups are triggered, and their demand satisfied, the final market participants to enter the market are the momentum traders. These traders are watching the market for signs of movement, and will take positions anytime they see the rate of change in price accelerate in the hopes that the market will continue to follow through. The trend bar that was forming attracts the momentum traders' attention and they begin to take their positions into the close. This aggressive buying helps to close the stock on its highs for the day and sets up a bullish environment for the following session.

Many bulls who missed the initial setup discover this stock as they scan after hours. They take entry the following day, and feel relieved that they were able to catch the stock before it left the station without them (see Figure 8.6). The following session, the market wiggles intraday and all of the traders who

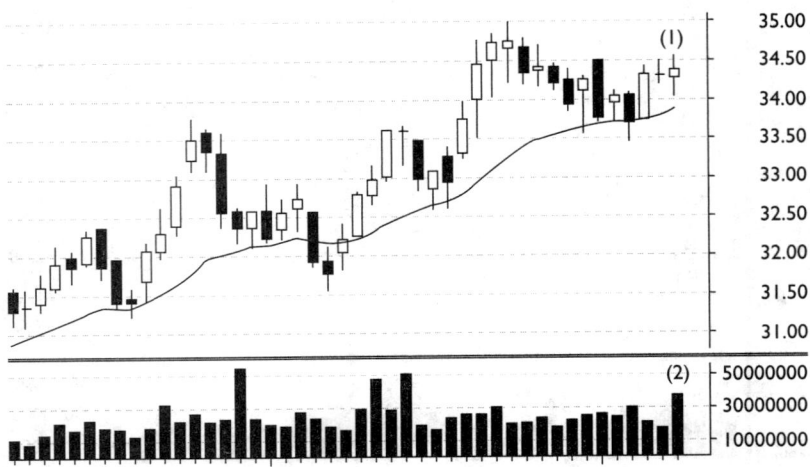

Figure 8.6

chickened out on their initial entry, or who for some reason missed the trade take this second chance to establish their long positions (1). You can see how many latecomers there were by the sharp increase in volume seen during this session (2).

All of these cascading bullish setups have triggered, and you can clearly see how the market responded as the bulls entered trades over the course of three sessions. However by the fourth day, there comes a point at which there are no more setups left. Every bullish strategy has triggered its orders, and those orders to buy have been filled. Demand, which had been hungry and insistent and willing to chase the price higher VANISHES!

If there is no demand, then by definition there must be an overabundance of supply. Thus, soon after the last bullish orders are filled, the supply/demand balance turns strongly bearish, and the price begins to fall.

As the selling pressure increases and price falls, there are very few bulls left to cushion its impact. Most of the bulls who were interested in this particular pattern have already taken their positions, and now as their setups seem to be failing there

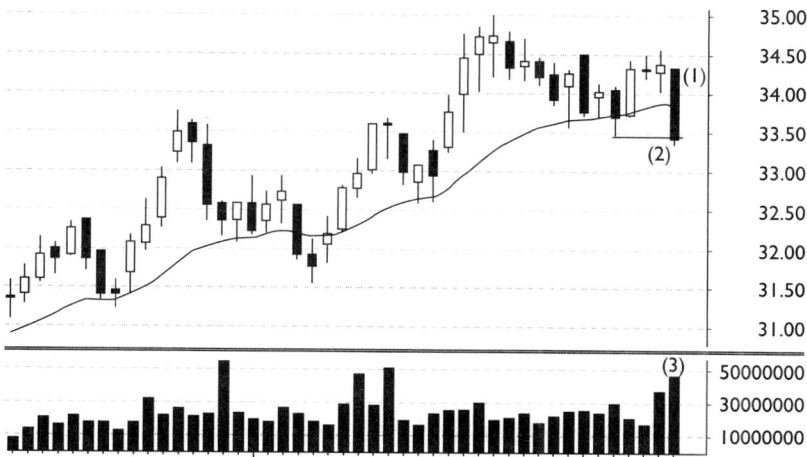

Figure 8.7

is little reason to consider adding shares (see Figure 8.7). The bid continues to be very weak, and the stock grinds steadily lower as price moves through the "air pocket" created by the recent cascade of bullish setups (1). Since the bulls are already positioned and the bid is thin, the nearest liquidity pool would likely be the area just below the last reversal bars lows (2). Since the majority of trading strategies use swing lows as their protective stop-loss point, we can be assured that there is an enormous cluster of stock market orders to sell placed just below the reversal bars low tick. As price breaks down to a new low, the stock market orders all go live at once. As they blindly compete for liquidity, the price quickly drops down and volume explodes as the stop market orders go live (3).

If you believe that the crowd is always wrong, then by definition you should be a buyer at the exact moment that their "wrongness" is proven! Remember, despite the recent pattern failures, the market is still trading within the context of a long term uptrend. So while the bullish rats flee the ship as the pullback pattern sinks into failure, the smart money

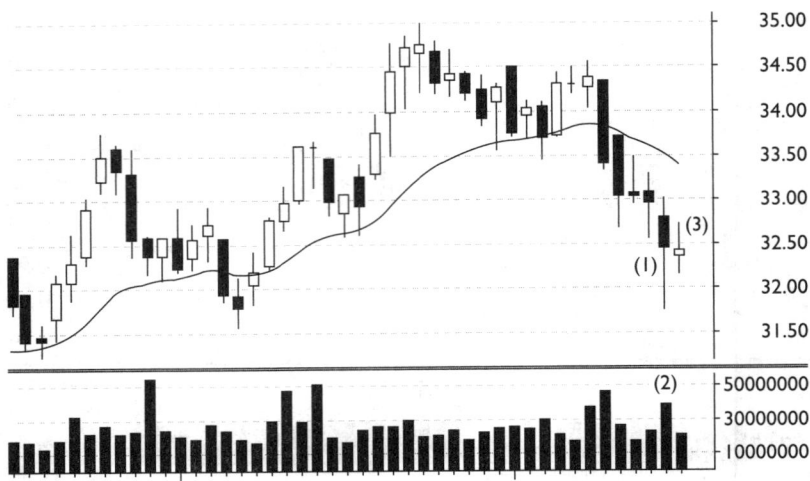

Figure 8.8

"sharks" circle slowly waiting for this selling micro-panic to reach a state of short term capitulation (see Figure 8.8; more on capitulation and euphoric market conditions in the next chapter). After five days of steady selling, the crowd finally gives up, and an extremely wide bar prints on the daily chart (1). This possible capitulation bar is confirmed by higher then average volume (2). and now that the crowd has been separated from their positions, the "rinse job" is complete. The following session an inside range bar forms, and acts as further confirmation that an important bottom has been reached (3). Traders who believe that the crowd is always wrong begin to take long exposure in anticipation of a resumption of the stocks long-term uptrend.

Figure 8.9 shows how after the smart money enters the stock market (1), the price rallies (2), wiggles (3), then reverses for real and begins to follow through for the second time (4). As the rally builds strength, all of the bullish crowds buy triggers begin to go off again. Each strategy's constituency starts buying again as their setups trigger, and prices rise as demand

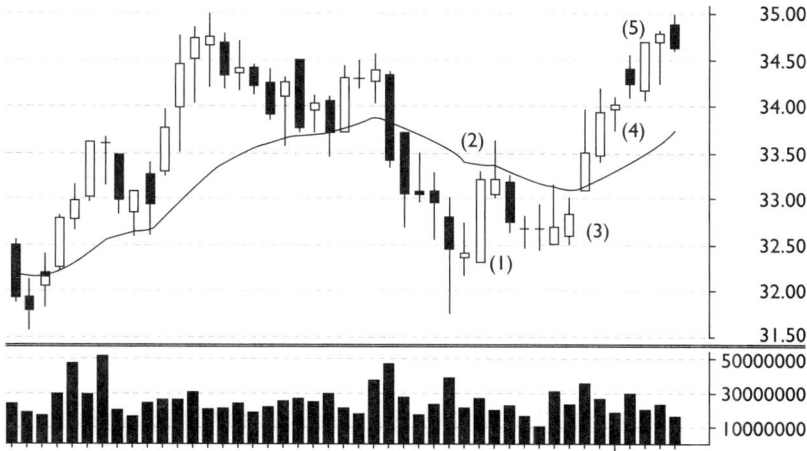

Figure 8.9

once again overcomes supply. As the recent whipsaw creates an environment without many excuses to short the market, price now pushes through an air pocket to the upside. With very little liquidity on the offer, the bulls must chase aggressively in order to get filled. Add to this dynamic, the traders who are watching in horror as the market screams back to the upside. Their bullish positions looked so good after the pullback, but then cost them money as the stop-loss orders were triggered during the rinse job.

Now the price is flying back up in the direction of their original opinion ... and they don't have any positions open to take advantage of this movement! They react emotionally, and frantically try to reestablish their original positions. Trade plans go out the window as these traders take shares simply in reaction to the pain and frustration they are feeling. This "revenge trading" adds a super aggressive stream of buy orders to an already unbalanced market. The market races back to the upside and eventually reaches the original pullback's profit objective near $35 per share (5)!

Insider's Advice   Traders with a complete understanding of the rinse cycle and its cause will dramatically outperform those speculators following a simple pattern recognition model. My favorite way to exploit a rinse is to use it as an entry trigger. If you believe as I do that the crowd is always wrong, then entering just as their stop-losses are triggering is the most elegant of entries. These aggressive entries offer a number of benefits.

Since you are fading into your positions against a breakdown/breakout, when your reversal opinion is proven wrong, your stop-loss orders will be triggered very quickly in the follow-through for the break point. These quick stop-losses will give your buying power back and will allow you to move on to the next trade when your opinions are disproved, and losses are taken. However, when your opinion is proven correct and there are profits to be taken, these aggressive entries will deliver the maximum risk-to-reward ratio possible for any given reversal.

During the day, I watch the time and sales window stream its order flow as the breakout/breakdown occurs. If there is a flurry of order flow after the break, and then the market goes silent, that is my trigger for entry. This is very much an issue of feel and experience, like hitting a baseball. With practice, you will be able to identify these shifts in market rhythm almost like the chord changes of a piece of music. For the swing/position trader who is operating on a deeper time frame, a "rinse job" entry can be triggered by a reversal bar on the daily chart. As soon as the pattern can be identified, an entry can be taken with a protective stop-loss order set just beyond the last high/low.

Figure 8.10 is an example of a rinse job entry (or "Peek" Reversal) from a chart of daily price action. The market becomes oversold as a wide bar forms (1) on much higher then

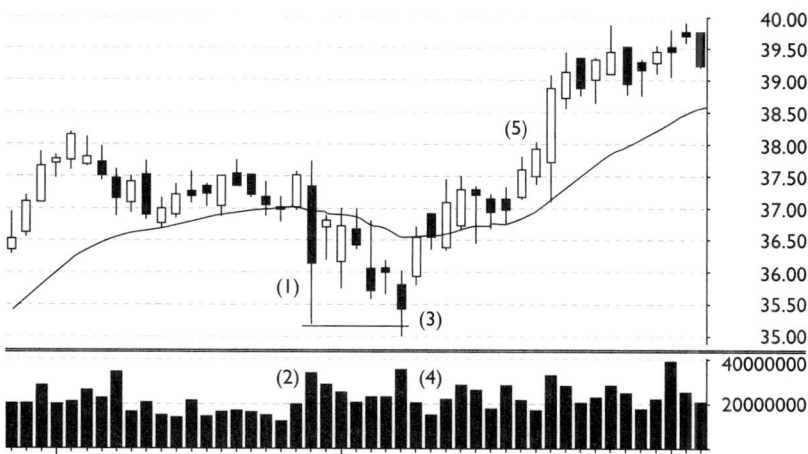

Figure 8.10 Example of a peek reversal

average volume (2). The crowd comes in to buy, and the stock
rallies for several days. Then as the technical buying surge
loses steam, the stock immediately heads down in the direction of the nearest liquidity pool. (The lows of the last reversal
bar.) As this liquidity pool is tested, the market breaks down
to a new low, then quickly reverses on a higher then average
volume (3), (4). The rinse now complete——the market turns
back to the bull side and rallies out to new highs (5).

CHAPTER 9

THE TRAP OF PATTERN RECOGNITION

*What we call chaos is just patterns we haven't recognized.
What we call random is just patterns we can't decipher. What
we can't understand we call nonsense. What we can't read we
call gibberish.*

—CHUCK PALAHNIUK

M ost of the educational material available to the modern speculator deals only with entries in terms of price patterns or "setups." However, another great way to exploit the crowd's magical aptitude for loss is to try and capture the movement surrounding the crowd's panic as a trading setup *fails*. Let's analyze the most basic technical setup in existence—the "pennant" or base near highs.

Pennant Pattern

After a market has experienced a strong rally, price will exhaust itself into some area of resistance. While this resistance is strong enough to halt the rally, it lacks the power to reverse the market. Rather than a bearish reversal and the beginnings of a correction, buyers and sellers slug it out in near perfect equilibrium. This balance of supply and demand creates a narrow trading range that shows up on a price chart as a horizontal bar or "pennant." If the bulls retain control of the market, eventually the overabundance of supply will be overcome. Then once the pool of liquidity that created price resistance has been soaked up, price will be free to break out to a new high.

Traditionally, a pennant pattern (see Figure 9.1) triggers its long entry when price breaks out above the highs of the range (1). Protective stop-loss levels are then set below the extreme low of the range (2). In a successful pennant, all of the bullish orders surrounding the breakout to a new high will create an extreme short-term demand imbalance in the market. The sharp increase in demand forces traders to chase supply up and up, and it is this behavior that produces the sharp bullish follow-through characteristic of a pennant style breakout.

However, if the market fails to react to the increase in bullish order flow, it tells us that there is a large level of hidden

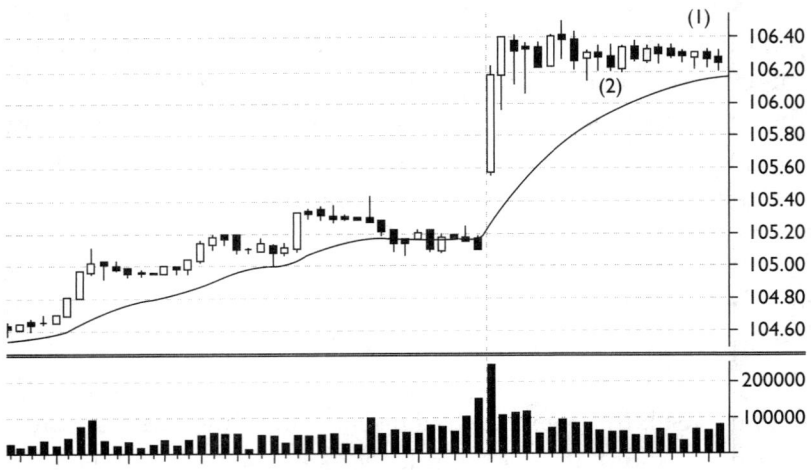

Figure 9.1 Example of a pennant pattern

supply in the market. This hidden supply is often a large market participant liquidating a position, and once their true intentions are revealed, they often abandon any subterfuge and begin selling in earnest. This is the reason why a false setup in a pennant pattern can often trigger an enormous wave of selling in smaller time frames. For the daily based, or intraday trader, these counter-intuitive "failure" trades often deliver more edge than the more traditional trend trading setups.

In Figure 9.2, the traditional trader enters a long position in reaction to the stock's breakout above its upper trend line (1), and sets his protective stop-loss order under the lows of the base (2). This entry/stop-loss pairing produces a risk of .40 per share. With a profit expectation of $1, (typical follow-through for a pennant pattern in a stock with a three digit share price.) this trade has a projected yield of 2.5 to 1.

The contrarian thinker or anti-crowd trader, isn't interested in the traditional breakout setup, but is constantly scanning a list of pennant patterns in the hopes that one of them will

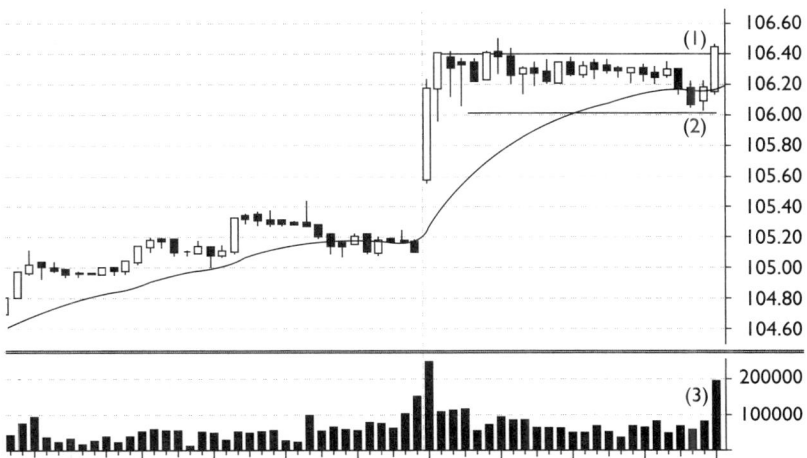

Figure 9.2

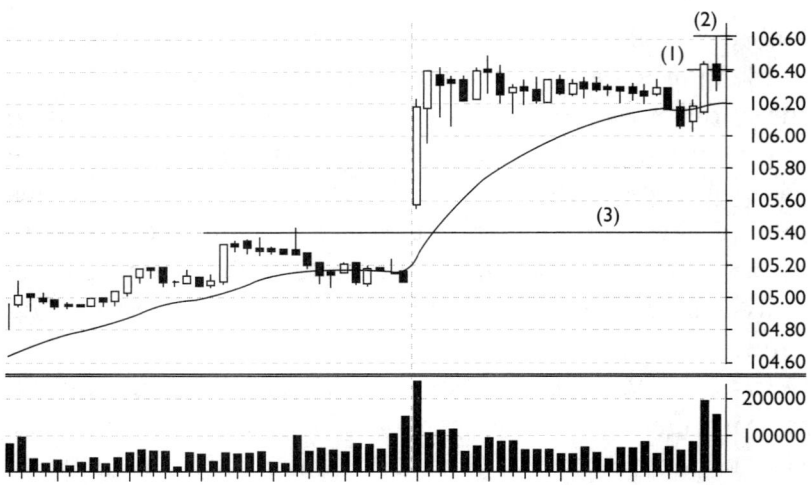

Figure 9.3

show signs of failure. If the crowd is all trading the pennant, they are likely to be wrong, and the true profit opportunity in the stock will be to the short side! When this pennant clearly breaks out to the upside and fails to follow through, he begins to watch this stock as a potential trade candidate (see Figure 9.3).

When the breakout bar closes as a reversal candlestick, the contrary thinker enters a short position (1), and sets a protective stop-loss level above the highs of the reversal candlestick (2). Because this trade is contrary in nature, the market should not exhibit the same whipsaw or rinse tendencies as described earlier. Also since the crowd isn't trading with a bearish bias, they will not have created the liquidity pools that would likely provoke a rinse job around that high. Therefore it is "safe" to use the high of the reversal candlestick as a stop-loss level. As we analyze this trade, you can see that it offers an initial risk of .20 per share. With an area of clear chart support at $105.40 per share (3), the trade has the potential to deliver a $1 profit for a 5 to 1 risk-to-reward ratio.

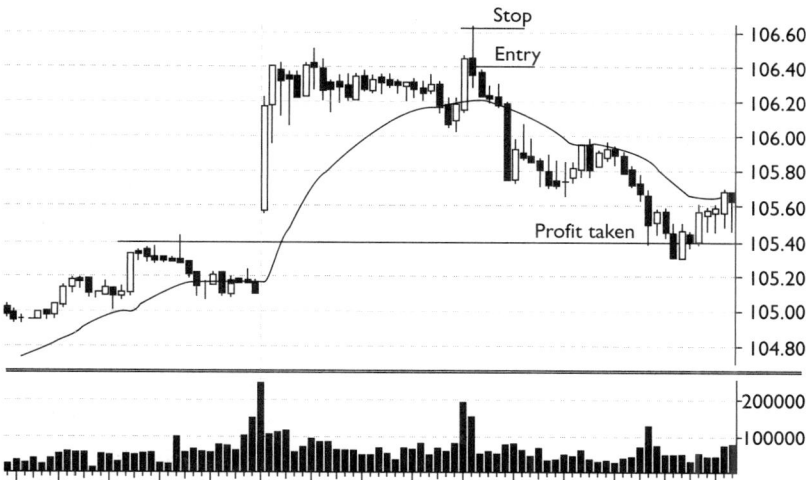

Figure 9.4 Example of a gopher trade

Gopher Trades

As luck would have it, the false breakout in the stock did indeed trigger a waterfall of selling that delivered that 5 to 1 profit by the time it exhausted itself into chart support near $105.40 (see Figure 9.4). This setup/failure price action is reminiscent of the old "Whack-a-Gopher" game seen at county fairs around the country. You are given a mallet, and are supposed to whack a small mechanical gopher as it pops its head up into the game area. This is why I have dubbed these breakout failures "gopher trades." Just like the carnival game, price pokes its head up beyond the breakout point and gets "whacked" soundly by the bears.

As you can see from these examples, trading with the crowd can offer *some* edge, but trading against it is a far richer proposition. If we focus on these two setups at the individual market participant level, we see that in order for the traditional breakout setup to produce a profit, many other traders must "agree" with our opinion that the market is about to rally.

A traditional breakout setup needs a flurry of new buy orders in order to sustain its rally long enough to reach profit objectives. Traders must take action and assume the risk of loss in order for a traditional breakout play to reach a profitable conclusion. When you trade a breakout in the traditional manner, you are "hoping" others will take action and ensure your success.

The contrarian trader enjoys a far superior position. Since the setup he is stalking can only form *after a breakout has occurred*, this trader knows that there is a crowd of buyers who have just entered bullish positions. For the gopher trade to be a success, traders must simply react in fear and scratch their already open positions as they see the pattern begin to disintegrate. Thus, the contrarian trader's setup is relying not on hope but instead on a clear knowledge of human psychology—avoidance of pain. Not only does the gopher trade offer a superior risk-to-reward ratio, but it offers an increased accuracy rate as well! After all, if you believe that the crowd is always wrong, then trading against them *must offer* superior profitability and edge to the informed speculator.

The liquidity pool theory that explains why a "rinse job" occurs can be directly targeted in a more positive manner to set up what I call a "magnet trade" situation. As previously stated, markets are drawn toward areas of high liquidity. When a stock, futures contract, or currency pairing forms a buy signal just below a large liquidity pool, it offers an extremely high probability trade for the knowledgeable speculator.

In Figure 9.5, any knowledgeable trader will recognize the buy signal generated by this market as it forms a base near highs or pennant pattern on its intraday chart (1). The crowd of traders will also identify an area of resistance overhead in the form of the 200-period simple moving average (2). The 200-period simple moving average is another technical indicator that is widely followed as a roving area of support or resistance. These

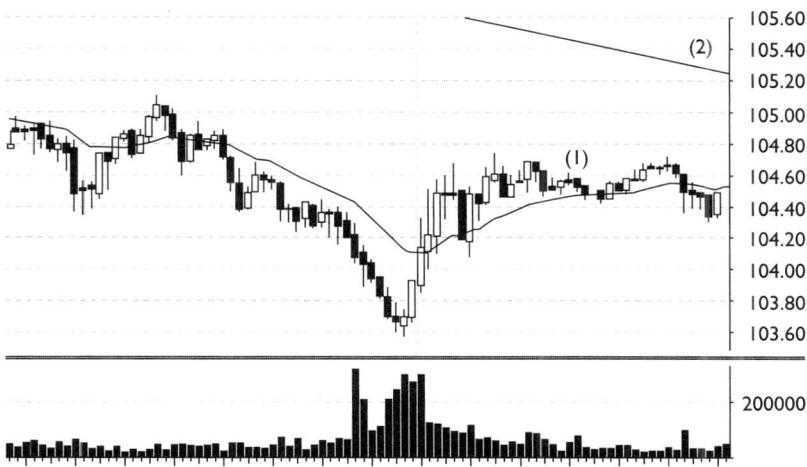

Figure 9.5 Example of an air pocket of illiquidity

two technical entities, a bullish price pattern and a technical level of resistance, create two areas of dense liquidity, with an "air pocket" of extreme *illiquidity* between them.

Magnet Trades

This "magnet trade" is essentially ping-pong movement between two liquidity pools. This is exactly the same scenario as a rinse job. In Figure 9.6, the air pocket between the two liquidity pools will be exploited as an asset, rather than defended against as a liability. To take advantage of a magnet trade, I like to initiate a position after a test of the range lows (1). I then set my protective stop-loss order at an arbitrary level far enough below the lows of the range (2) to avoid any whipsaw losses due to "normal" volatility. (One stop-loss sizing strategy I like personally is to estimate the average width of the last 10 candlesticks, and use that number as my arbitrary stop.) As soon as the position is taken and the stop-loss order goes live, I place a limit order to take profits just below the 200 period moving average (3).

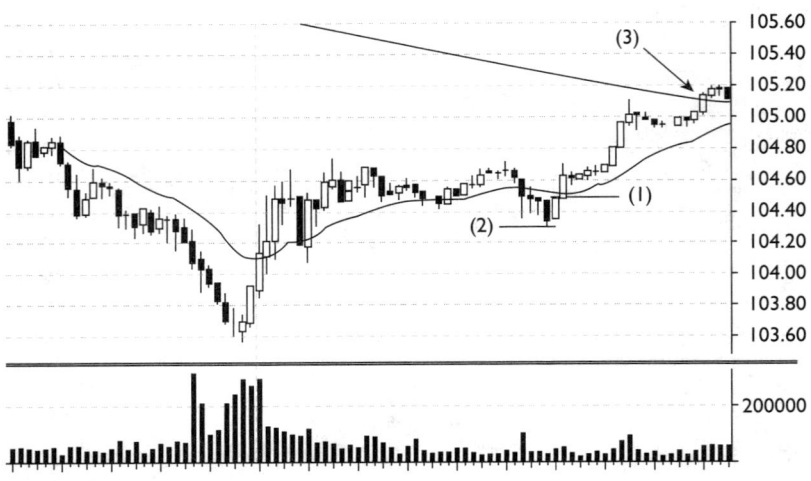

Figure 9.6 Example of a magnet trade

As you can see from the chart, the magnet trade is a fairly solid strategy. Before you take a position, you know where entry, stop-loss, and profit objective orders will be placed. Most brokers who serve the active trader community offer the ability to input "bracketed orders." A limit order to open the position is tied to a stop market order and limit order to sell the same contracts when either stop-loss or profit objective levels are tested. This creates a broker managed order set that allows the trader to leave his computer and pursue other interests while the magnet trade works away in the background.

While writing this chapter, I noticed that the U.S. dollar versus the Japanese yen pairing in the foreign currency markets had pulled back to test an area of chart support on its hourly chart.

This setup has nothing to do with either the 20 or 200 period moving averages, yet nonetheless it was a classic magnet trade. Classic technical analysis teaches that prior areas of support become resistance when retested (see Figure 9.7). Therefore, I felt a large number of bearish market participants would be laying in wait to put on short positions as resistance near 119.20

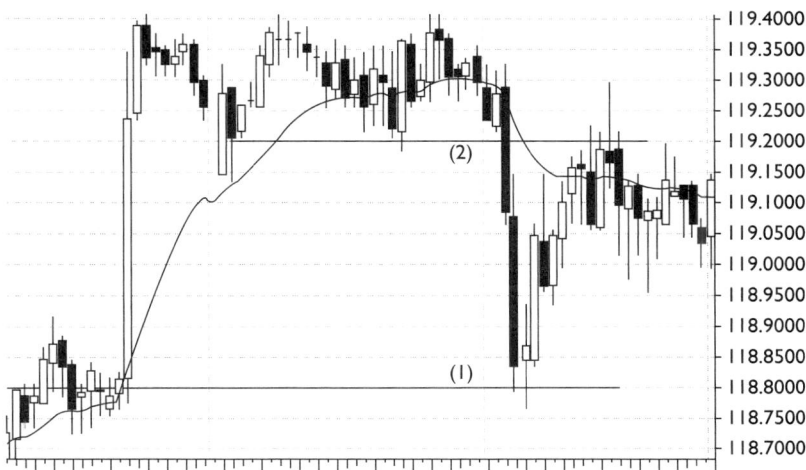

Figure 9.7

was tested (2). If support near 118.80 could hold (1), then I felt sure the liquidity pool created by the waiting bears would create a large air pocket of low liquidity between these two levels. (Since I was busy writing), I entered a limit order to convert $300,000 into yen as support was tested near 118.80. I linked this order to a stop market order to convert my yen back into dollars if the price were to continue its decline and test the 118.60 level. I also linked a limit order to convert my yen back into dollars if the price were to rally up the chart to test resistance near 119.20. With these orders in place, I turned back to my writing and completely ignored my trading screens.

Soon thereafter, I heard the sound alert of an order being executed, and found that my initial limit order had been filled. After double checking to make sure that both my stop market order and limit order to take profits were correct and live on my broker's book, I again went back to my work. Many hours later, I heard the alert sound again and looked over to see that the market had rallied after testing support and had indeed zoomed up through its air pocket to test resistance. As you can see from the chart itself, this resistance was strong enough to turn the price lower as the Bears began to take control of the trend.

Looking back at the chart, my magnet trade has already been buried by the noise. This setup produced approximately 35 "pips" of profit, or 1.75 to 1 off my initial 20 pips of risk. With an initial position size of $300,000, each pip was worth a little more than $25, so an $880 profit was realized while I was *fully engaged on an entirely different project!* This is one of the beauties of trading as a business. It is true that the learning curve can be difficult and steep. But once you achieve competency, trading can be a very part-time job with a very full-time paycheck.

Reading a Chart's Storyline

By analyzing which constituencies from the technical analysis trading community are active in a given market, you can develop trading strategies with probabilities that simple pattern recognition alone can never produce. As you develop your chart reading skills, each new chart will unfold before you like a storyboard of supply and demand.

Think of traditional technical analysis as a young child learning to read. He pours over the page, excitedly pointing and exclaiming each time an individual word is recognized. The chart reader looks at the same page, and doesn't notice the individual words, sentences, or paragraphs. Instead each paragraph is read in a flash, and it is the storyline and character situations that jump off the page. Every time I look at a new chart, I'm reading its storyline. If I notice that the last three pullback trades worked to perfection for all traditional entry strategies, this tells me that there is an established crowd showing open profits on their bullish positions.

The more crowd traders involved in a stock, the better I can predict its future movements as well as the panic trigger points

Insider's Advice Learn as much as you can about traditional trading techniques and technical analysis, then use this knowledge *against* those market participants who have yet to learn to see *what is really going on* in a price chart.

most likely to produce an implosion. The stock has a built-in "death dive" based on its current friendliness to the traditional technical analyst. Remember, the crowd always loses, therefore when they experience a period of profitability, it is such a welcome relief from their consistent failure that they tend to be hyperdefensive of their open profits. Eventually, when one of these pullbacks runs out of steam and turns into a pattern failure, it is likely to trigger a rather hysterical wave of selling as the uninformed crowd blunders away from their long exposure.

By now, you should be able to see how that storyline jumped out at me from Figure 9.8. Can you also spot the trading opportunity I saw to exploit the predictability and profit potential of a panicking crowd?

Figure 9.8

MONITOR YOUR HIGHS AND LOWS

Everyone gets what they want out of the markets …

—ED SEYKOTA

Speculation in financial markets is essentially the monetization of human activity. Like falling in love, having a family, starting a new career, it is filled with extreme highs and extreme lows. These emotional swings can be enormously destructive to your health, lifestyle, and relationships if not understood and actively managed. One of the most important tasks I seek to accomplish with my consulting clients is to teach them how to integrate their trading as part of a healthy and balanced life. We all want to be happy, and trading can provide for many of our basic needs which give one the time to seek true happiness. However, the majority of my trading clients exhibit strong signs of obsessive or addictive behavior surrounding the markets.

Behavioral Motivation

The root of all good and evil in our minds is the neurotransmitter dopamine. Dopamine is released in the brain to reward and motivate us as its presence creates strong feelings of pleasure and satisfaction. When you eat a particularly delicious piece of food, see a loved one after a long absence, win a hard-fought sporting event, it is dopamine that takes you to your "happy place." Dopamine IS pleasure/happiness/satisfaction in its chemical form.

In a natural state, this dopamine response system drives behavior in directions that would help you live a longer life and successfully propagate the species. But as we all know, the lifestyle of modern man has little to do with natural states. We have learned how to manipulate our pleasure centers with chemicals and behaviors, and these endeavors can play havoc with our decision-making process. The feelings of satisfaction and well-being that dopamine create are so strong and fundamental that in extreme cases the brain can ignore its basic drive for self preservation in an effort to experience these pleasures.

When a person ingests the drug cocaine, it binds to the dopamine in your system and artificially increases its concentration in your system. The drug taker experiences "pure pleasure" for a short amount of time, and the memory of this feeling motivates them to seek it again and again. But, by taking a drug, this person has hijacked his body's natural motivational system—a system whose purpose is behavior motivation and reward. In the natural state, when the human animal stumbles across a behavior that is "good," the brain rewards it mightily by dumping dopamine into the system. This powerful surge of pleasure gets your attention and motivates you to repeat the same behavior in the future.

This simple behavioral feedback loop makes perfect sense, but holds a fatal flaw. What if primitive man's brain reacted the same way every time he ate some tasty berries? If his body identified them as particularly nutritious, his brain would reward him with a dump of dopamine. If this were a static system, then this primitive animal might obsessively eat berries to the exclusion of everything else in an attempt to keep pleasure/satisfaction levels high. For this reason, the brain has a sliding scale of pleasure in response to repeated pleasurable behavior. When you first discover a new behavior that induces a pleasurable response, dopamine levels are extremely high. However, each subsequent time you repeat the behavior that brought you the initial surge of pleasure, you are now anticipating the pleasure that is to follow.

Since your brain is hardwired to reward *unexpected pleasures* with more intensity, thus motivating exploration, your dopamine levels fall progressively as less dopamine is released each time the behavior is repeated. With a reduced reward of pleasure/satisfaction the event loses its excitement factor, and your motivation to repeat it diminishes. This cycle of reduced dopamine response is what motivates us to keep seeking new experiences.

The logic of this behavioral motivation loop makes perfect sense when you think about it in terms of basic needs like food, shelter, and procreation. But when we take these behavioral motivations into a virtual world such as the financial marketplaces, the brain almost always sends out the wrong signals at the worst possible times. In one now famous study, monkeys' dopamine levels were monitored during tasks that involved risk and reward. The monkeys received a visual stimulus, and were then supposed to react to that event by pulling a lever. In one phase of the experiment, certain colors were shown, and when the monkey pulled the lever, a reward was given. In a second experiment, another color was shown and when the monkey pulled the lever, no reward was given. In the third and most important experiment, a third color was shown, and when the monkey pulled its lever, a reward was given randomly half the time.

The results of these experiments showed that dopamine levels were elevated only the first few times that the monkey correctly identified a certain color with a guaranteed reward. After the first few rewards were given, the monkey understood the stimulus/response relationship, and expected the reward. (In the first experiment the reward was always given.) Because of the behavioral feedback loop described earlier, dopamine levels steadily fell with each occurrence of the expected reward. Interestingly enough, in the second experiment dopamine levels rose with similar intensity as the monkey began to realize that while one color produced a consistent reward, the other color produced nothing. It can be said that the monkey was experiencing the joy of learning, and the scientists were able to show that spikes in dopamine levels were similar whether or not a reward was present. I believe this is why some traders love the research/learning aspects of strategy development, but fail miserably when it comes to strategy implementation. They are seeking the surge of good feelings that come from the identification of a new pattern, but are not really all that interested in what can be done with the pattern itself.

The most important and fascinating experiment from the monkey study was the third one. In this experiment, the color shown would only produce a reward 50 percent of the time, and would do so in a purely random manner. Because the monkey could never know for certain whether the next pull of the lever would offer a reward or not, it became obsessed as it tried in vain to discover a pattern to the rewards. It continually pulled the lever in a vain attempt to discern a pattern. Its dopamine levels rose every time it saw the random reward color, and spiked intensely each time when random luck delivered a reward. But even when the randomizer gave it no reward, the monkeys' dopamine levels would spike simply in *anticipation of potential reward!*

Profitable Trading Is *Boring*

Since we are motivated to find ways to keep dopamine levels high, we will go to great lengths to find and repeat the behaviors and experiences that make us feel good. I believe this is the reason why traders tend to flit from strategy to strategy, never remaining consistently profitable. Take it from a voice of experience—profitable trading is *enormously boring*. You have an edge, no one trade can make or break you, and you simply must put the time in it takes to grind out your profit for the month. In addition, a good trading program will have a solid trading plan behind it. All of the stressful situations that might arise have been analyzed previously and thus the randomized "thrill" has been taken out of the equation. Since the monkey study proved that we are hardwired to obsessively seek out new patterns in our world, traders would often rather seek out a new edge, (invent, create, innovate.) rather than exploit a known one (manual labor, repetitive tasks, paperwork!).

Discovering patterns and finding quirky ways to exploit these tendencies is what we as human beings are hardwired to do with our lives. This is why we enjoy the creative process, and often spend our leisure time learning, building, painting, drawing, creating etc. In my opinion, the drive to recognize patterns is a basic brain need, and is what drives the video game industry into a multi billion dollar worldwide endeavor. I believe this is why a ridiculously simple and repetitive game such as Tetris can be so tremendously satisfying.

Understanding how your brain is wired, and how its basic processes motivates you is important information for the financial speculator. Once you know and understand the processes of thought that guide your own trading motivations, you can begin to take that knowledge and use it to exploit the illogical motivations of other market participants. Neuroscience is likely the reason why stocks that surprise during earnings season exhibit "irrational exuberance" or depression, while stocks that meet expectations tend not to respond, or even move in a counter trend manner.

The increased reaction surrounding an unexpected event is what drives the superior profitability of the anticrowd trading strategies we discussed earlier. While a market may grind higher over time in reaction to a trend continuation pattern, it is much more likely to exhibit a quick and violent downdraft if an "unexpected" pattern failure forms. Put in simplest terms, the speculator seeks to profit by acquiring another market participant's risk. Logically, that market participant would only be willing to sell her position if she felt that her risk has little reward potential. If she was correct, then the speculator is the "greater fool" for purchasing her shares/contracts/exposure. Profitable speculation may exist because emotions, ego, and other chemical and biological motivations cause market participants to make inordinately poor decisions when the markets are at extremes.

Trade Capitulation *(When Possible)*

"Capitulation" is the term used to describe a market that has declined sharply and is producing extreme fear in the hearts of traders/investors. Fear is perhaps the most powerful emotion inherent to the market experience. It is fear that drives the investing public to sell their shares at a remarkable discount to "true value." When a market declines violently, the psychological pain these losses create often provoke the uninformed investors to react defensively as their illogical hysteria builds.

Let's follow the mindset of the average investor through a capitulation cycle in the major market indexes.

For the first few months of the trading year, this daily chart in Figure 10.1 of a major market index was happily rallying within the context of a stable uptrend. Each time areas of moving average support were tested, the bulls entered the market in droves and the trend resumed. Investors were happy, complacent, and profitable. Then a news event swept through the market which forced many investors to question their bullish bias.

The initial wave of selling was caused by those who believed that the day's news had brought the rally to an end. These sell orders stacked up before the market opened, and caused a large gap to the downside at the opening bell. This unexpected gap brought in more selling, as traders logged in and discovered to their horror how much of their paper profits had vanished. Because of the morning's news, most of the bulls had pulled their orders, and so all of the morning's sell side order flow was met with an extremely weak bid. This combination of weak demand/strong supply forced the market lower with increasing violence.

Figure 10.1

Each time the market bottomed during the day, a wave of hope would sweep through the trading community. Some traders hoped the market had bottomed and began to buy in anticipation of a bounce. Investors with established long positions hoped that the market had bottomed and that the subsequent rally would replace the paper profits they lost during the downdraft. Each time the market broke down to a new low, it dashed the hopes that had built up, and provoked another wave of selling from traders as well as established investors. Any intraday speculators trying to pick a bottom would likely have placed stops below the low of the day, so their stop market orders would be joining the investors' sell orders in a fight for fills that further increased the violence of each sell off.

This cycle of ever increasing fear and hysteria is analogous to the hand cranked siren of an antique fire engine. Each rotation of the handle raises the pitch and intensity of the siren's wail until it reaches a level of shrillness that hurts one's ears. When a market reaches that same extreme, the majority of market participants throw-up their hands, and are convinced that the market will continue to go down indefinitely. They have watched as enormous amounts of money vanish from their brokerage accounts, and are certain that the losses have only just begun. This feeling of certain doom provokes them to contact their brokers and sell "at any price." When this occurs, capitulation is at hand, and the market will often experience one last surge to the downside.

When a wave of selling gains momentum and becomes hysterical, the informed and experienced speculator remains objective and waits for capitulation to mature. He knows that the crowd is always wrong. Therefore, if he can identify the final wave of selling into capitulation, an entry can be taken at the exact moment in which the crowd abandons the market. Again, it is the reality of the liquidity cycle that makes this a profitable entry point.

As negative emotions reach an extreme, there will come a point where the crowd tries to sell at once. During this capitulatory phase, the market will overshoot radically to the downside until it finds a level at which prices are so cheap that traders are motivated to buy in spite of the market's negative expectations. Once this buying (demand) overcomes the crowd's selling (selling), the market halts and total capitulation has been reached.

The market then reverses violently and shoots up almost as hysterically as it had recently dropped. This is due to the fact that during the capitulation cycle, all traders with shares to sell unloaded their positions in a mad rush. Now that the market has bottomed, and the signs of reversal are attracting bullish interest there are very few shares left on the offer. The bulls must therefore compete with one another for fills as they all chase the price higher. The "air pocket" created by capitulation now fills and generates a quick and very rich profit for the those traders who bought shares in anticipation of a bounce.

As an informed speculator, your job is to define when the market reaches its peak of hysteria and then consider taking long exposure in anticipation of the bounce that will follow. Figure 10.2 illustrates a classic situation cycle that played itself out within the context of one trading day.

The day started out with a reasonable amount of strength. A bullish price thrust in the morning session exhausted itself around 10:00am and the market began to base near its highs in what should be a familiar pennant or base near highs pattern (1). After the noontime doldrums, the bulls came back to the market and the price rallied to break out above the highs of the range (2). This bullish price action would have triggered the technical trading crowd's buy orders, and this opinion could have been confirmed by noting the spike in volume as the trigger point was tested (3). The market wiggled after its breakout, and then formed a lower high as the breakout

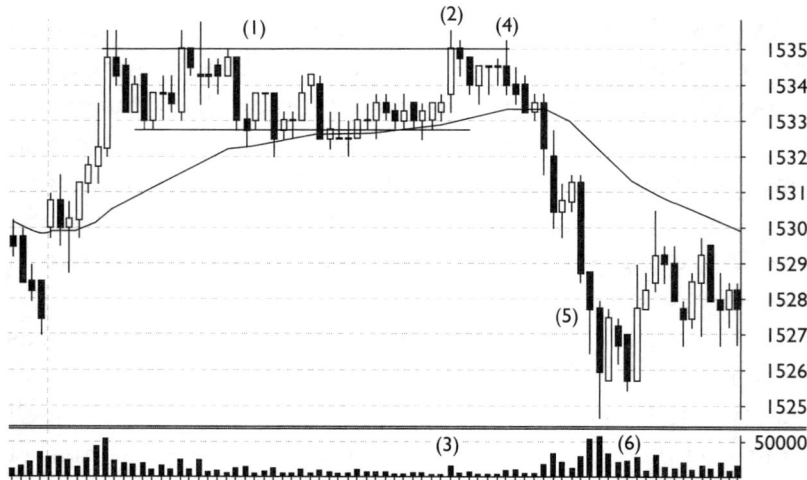

Figure 10.2

point was retested (4). This breakout failure proved to be the trigger point for bullish panic as the market began to steadily accelerate to the downside.

After a period of sustained selling, the bulls began to get scared. They started to blow out their positions, and the "sell at any costs" behavior caused several high volatility candlesticks to form (5). As this volatility reached an extreme, volume exploded and printed its highest levels of the session (6). Radical bar expansion coupled with extraordinary volume is the hallmark of capitulation, and as you can see, those extremes created a sustainable low for the session.

Market Euphoria

Euphoria is the exact opposite of capitulation. If you replace every cycle of fear just discussed with a cycle of greed, a market will experience the same ramped acceleration culminating in a "blow off" top. I prefer to trade capitulation whenever possible because in my experience markets tend to overshoot far more to the downside then they do when blowing out in a bullish manner. During capitulation, traders are selling shares they already own. They are reducing their market risk—risk that they currently are exposed to. For a market to experience euphoria, traders must be convinced that there is little to no downside risk, and that they will miss out on enormous windfall profits if they fail to participate in the rally. Humans are naturally pessimistic creatures, therefore it is much easier for a market to convince them that they are about to lose their life savings, and much harder to convince them that they will double their net worth if they just buy that one "hot stock."

It is for this psychological reason that I try to find fear-based trades even when a market is experiencing euphoria. When a market capitulates, I am aggressively taking exposure in anticipation of a bounce. But when a market goes euphoric, I rarely try to pick its top. Instead I will wait for the market to print a signal of trend failure. These reversal patterns are so well-known and widely followed that they almost always provoke a strong fear response from the traders who may have been insanely bullish just a short time ago. I find these whipsaw fear responses to be much more predictable, and that they produce a much larger risk-to-reward ratio then the euphoric event itself.

My favorite reversal pattern has to be a variation on the double top, and I have termed it a "peek reversal." This reversal pattern forms when a market experiences euphoria, then falls back down to test areas of support. The bearish reversal must be clean enough, and the decline large enough to attract bearish attention and trigger short signals for the crowd. Their sell orders drive the market lower, but this need for liquidity on the bid is soon satisfied. Less experienced traders who missed out on the sharp rally that preceded euphoria see this pullback as a buying opportunity, and begin to establish "second chance" long positions.

This buying pressure pushes the market up into the air pocket created by the short sales of the bears, and in an instant the market moves back up to retest its previous high. Since most reversal based trading strategies use prior highs/lows in order to set protective stop-loss levels, it is almost a sure thing that there is a large liquidity pool present a few ticks above the highs. This liquidity pool draws the price up for a breakout, and as soon as the price breaks above its previous high, the stop-loss orders go active and the market surges higher under the strain.

Since euphoria is a usually violent event, there will be many bears who missed out on the chance to get short, and will fade any breakout with thanks that the market offered them a second chance to get short. Since the rally to the breakout point is usually driven by inexperienced second chance bulls, there often is little size driving the rally. As the bears begin to apply pressure, these bulls react in fear to the failed breakout. (In other words, the market only "peeked" its head up above the prior high before quickly reversing.)" *Blast it, I got suckered again!"* they exclaim as they pound their sell keys in an attempt to stem their losses. This aggressive selling into an already weak bid sends the market sharply lower, and is the real reason why this pattern is one of my all-time favorites.

Psychology of a Peek Reversal

Since you are fading a breakout to a new high in anticipation of trend failure, you will know very quickly if your entry was a good one or not. If the market continues to trend to the upside, thus confirming the validity of the breakout, then your protective stop-loss order will trigger and your loss will be quickly taken. If the market reverses hysterically after the false breakout reveals itself, your trade profits will accumulate quickly and dramatically as the market implodes. This immediacy of feedback lowers your stress, and ensures that your capital remains tied up only in trades that are working in your favor. Since a peek reversal failure triggers stop-loss orders very quickly, any losses will be taken quickly and your capital will be free for the next trading opportunity.

Figure 10.3, shows a strong market experiencing euphoria and forms a simple pivot reversal to the downside (1). This halts the rally, and attracts profit takers and bearish traders who sell shares into the air pocket created by the "buy only" greed of euphoria. As soon as this technically triggered surge of selling has pushed the price down until supply is satisfied, the market halts (2). Since the selling just experienced was technically driven, it too creates an air pocket on the chart (3). As inexperienced bulls blindly react to a small–time-frame pullback, they must compete for the few shares that exist on the offer. This drives price back up towards the previous high, and eventually triggers the bears' stop-loss orders as the price breaks out above $42 per share area (4).

The majority of these protective stop-loss orders will be in the form of stop market orders, and therefore will create a "buy

Figure 10.3

at any price" surge of order flow. This drives the price higher, and suckers in the breakout buying constituencies active in the marketplace. As soon as their demand for shares is satisfied, yet another air pocket has been created (5)! As we have seen in the other examples, once the breakout fails and the fear level of the bulls rises, the market experiences a sharp supply/demand imbalance and price falls violently as the peek reversal short reaches its profit objectives (6).

As you look back over this case study, you can see how many different constituencies must act upon poorly analyzed information in order to form a peek reversal pattern. I strongly believe that the peek reversal's powerful profitability is directly related to the many mistakes that are made in the bars preceding the "smart money" entry point. When trading this pattern on an intraday chart, I watch the order flow in real time and initiate my short position in the pause that follows the breakout's surge of liquidity. This is the same skill set I described earlier when speaking of the entry strategy for a false breakout of a pennant. You wait for the flow of buy orders to pause, and fill your short position in the lull between continuation or reversal.

When looking for peek reversals in deeper time frames, I look for any reversal candlesticks that form immediately after the stock/futures contract/foreign currency pair breaks out to a new high.

In Figure 10.4, you can clearly see how this up trending market moved into euphoria as it tested the $17.50 per share area (1). Then the requisite pullback formed over the next four sessions (2). The market then worked its way higher, and broke out to a new high and immediately reversed not once, but *twice in a row* (3)! With the peek reversal pattern showing clearly on the daily chart, a short trade would have been initiated the following morning at the open. Since a peek reversal can be thought

Figure I0.4

of as the whipsaw of a whipsaw of a whipsaw——protective stop-loss orders would have been placed just above the highs around $17.50. You can then see how quickly and violently the stock followed through as the fear this pattern seeks to capture swept through the marketplace.

As we have established previously, people want to feel good as they trade. But I hope by now I have illustrated to you how "good feelings" are more likely the identifying signals of a *negative edge* rather than a positive one. So enter the laboratory with a predatory mindset, and look for market behaviors that induce negative feelings (profitable) rather than positive feelings (unprofitable). In doing so, you are harnessing powerful cycles of brain chemistry induced emotions for monetary gain rather than personal satisfaction; so many of my consulting clients have come to me after falling into this trap. They forget that they trade to make the money they need in order to increase levels of personal satisfaction in their life *outside the markets*.

Control Your Stress Response

Another aspect of our human neurochemistry, which has a direct relationship to speculative profitability, is the stress response. When confronted with a negative experience, our nervous system begins to release two hormones into our brain. The first, widely known as adrenaline (also known as epinephrine), while the second hormone cortisol, isn't as commonly understood by the general public.

Since the human animal would have faced many physical threats in a primitive environment, the stress response is intended to enhance short-term physical performance so that we can better fight or flee from a dangerous situation. Adrenaline and cortisol divert blood away from less vital organs, increase blood sugar and glycogen levels so that your muscles will have more fuel with which to operate, and increase heart rate and respiration so that you may physically operate at a much higher level of intensity. As any serious athlete can tell you, all of these hormonal responses work extremely well to increase one's ability to perform physical tasks.

But a trader isn't fighting a woolly mammoth or running from a saber tooth tiger. Instead, they spend their days sitting in comfy chairs in an air-conditioned office watching pixels twitter back-and-forth on a computer screen. Our biological stress response is therefore grossly mismatched to the task at hand. Another dirty little biological secret is the fact that increased adrenaline and cortisol levels produce impaired cognitive performance! These hormones have been pumping into your system so that you can fight hard, and run fast. Deep strategic thought is not part of the plan! It is for this reason that speculators must learn to manage/reduce stress in order to maintain health, and most importantly *reduce trading errors.*

When I first began to understand the negative relationship between my hormonal stress response and my trading results,

I tried many different methods to manage my stress. Some helped, most did not, and all of them left me feeling fairly foolish! My particular problem was cognitive dysfunction. I was day trading stocks at the time, and was required to analyze enormous quantities of data in real time. This was hard work during the quietest sessions, and my inexperience made it all the more difficult. I would get enormously stressed, and as my adrenaline and cortisol levels peaked, I would get flummoxed and make enormously basic trading errors that sharply eroded my edge in the markets. The impaired cognitive performance the scientists described when writing about stress response was my biggest nemesis.

I kept trying different stress control ideas, but never found anything that worked satisfactorily for me. Then one day it hit me. It was ridiculous for me to think that I could control an innate biological function of my brain. Instead of fighting my hormones, I needed to find a way to work *with them* to achieve my goals. After that, when my trading made me feel stressed, and I identified the symptoms as my *adrenalized nervous system*, I did exactly what my body expected me to do ... fight or flight! I would get out of my comfy chair and do something quick and physical to burn off the stress hormones.

Insider's Advice   This simple biologically aligned stress management technique can be adopted by any trader. Just find some high-intensity physical activity that will increase your heart rate and burn off the increased blood sugar and glycogen from your muscles. Not only will it help your physical and mental health, but you'll be surprised how focused your trading will become. The mental errors and outright mistakes that are common in the beginning years of your trading career will vanish and your precision in execution and attention to detail will dramatically increase.

I soon found that a couple minutes of high-intensity push-ups, running up and down several flights of stairs, or a jog around the block was all it took to burn off the negative hormones and restore my cognitive and emotional balance.

CHAPTER 11

WHAT KIND OF TRADER ARE YOU?

Knowing others is intelligence; knowing yourself is true wisdom. Mastering others is strength; mastering yourself is true power.

—TAO TE CHING

By now I hope you are beginning to understand how much your success or failure as a trader revolves around your inner growth and development rather than external entities such as markets, systems, strategies. There are more edge filled strategies than you could trade in 20 lifetimes, yet many traders waste their career looking for the holy grail of "the perfect strategy." The truth is that every strategy will have its own unique cyclicality, markets that fit it perfectly, (payout cycles) and markets in which it delivers universal failure (payback cycles). With all my experience working with traders from every walk of life, I have come to believe that there are three tests one must pass in order to become a long-term, profitable trader.

Test Number One—Surviving Long Enough to Achieve Competency

The first and most important test is that the beginning trader must survive long enough to achieve competency. The failure rate for traders is staggering. I remember hearing a statistic when I first started trading that has always stuck with me.

Eighty percent of traders quit or fail within six months. Of the 20 percent who survive, 80 percent will have left the business within five years.

My experience as a teacher and consultant leads me to believe that the majority of traders fail because they disrespected the trading process. They see trading as "easy money," and start trading aggressively before they understand how to analyze edge and have proven their profitability. When I speak before trading audiences around the world, I try to communicate how important it is to respect the market's ability to do harm to one's portfolio. I talk about treating trading as a business, whether or not you intend it to be your primary source of income. As you might expect, the reality-based aspects of these presentations rarely resonate with a crowd of uninformed beginners. Having listened to me, they will head out to hear another speaker who promises them riches, cars, and sex appeal by next Thursday if they only buy the huff-and-puff trading system. They purchase these products, and lose a great deal of money floundering around as they trade with the crowd. Four to six months later, my phone rings as they realize the truth of my words. My typical retail client has lost 30 percent to 50 percent of their trading account by the time they come to me for consulting or attend a seminar.

If they started their trading with $100,000 in their account, they had enough capital to expect to live off their trading proceeds alone. Now they only have $50,000 left, and even if

I transform them into the best traders in the world, their new-found skills will barely cover the rent. I can remember four individuals I worked with last year who learned to trade with great skill and effectiveness, but left the business because they simply didn't have the capital needed to let trading alone pay their bills. I can only hope that they understand that their failure was not one of skill, but of timing. Hopefully they will come back to the markets once they are properly capitalized and enjoy the success their skills deserve.

Test Number Two—Achieving Consistency in Returns

If the first test is simply survival, then the second test would have to be consistency. Many traders fail to achieve consistent returns because they are constantly in search of a better edge. They stumble over the stacks of $100 bills that their current strategies could produce in a vain attempt to find their own definition of a Holy Grail trade. As I have mentioned before, the key to increasing your earning power as a trader lies not in trade frequency, or number of markets followed, but in the amount of risk one assumes *plus* the average risk-to-reward ratio of the strategy being traded. If you have a profitable trading strategy that delivers three units of profit a month with consistency, then you can double your monthly income by simply doubling your initial risk.

The traders I know personally who have been trading for 20 years or more have been trading the same way for decades. They have a few core strategies that work for them and their personalities. They press these edges with maximum effectiveness and very large position sizes in order to enjoy a seven-figure income each year. Trading is very much like chess— slightly illogical and complicated to learn at first—but once the rules are mastered, it is an incredibly simple game with endless strategic possibilities. It is not the board or pieces that make the game difficult, it is only the brain of your opponent that can challenge and confound.

Test Number Three—Learning Flexibility (Do Not Fear Change)

The third test that halts many traders' progress is just a rigidity of thought and action. The world's financial markets are comprised of human beings from different backgrounds and cultures interacting in real time to discover the correct price for any given instrument. A trader's road to profitability can be so long and psychologically painful that once consistent profitability has been achieved, that edge becomes the object of reverence and worship. These rigid traders find their edge, and make a great deal of money while their edge persists because of their near religious devotion to their rules. But the markets are constantly changing their character and behavioral tendencies, so sooner or later every edge will lose its effectiveness. A trader who is unwilling to change strategies when the market moves away from his/her edge, will give back the majority of the money made during his/her profitable years. It is this tendency toward rigidity and fear of change that I believe causes the majority of traders to lose, burnout, and quit the business after three to five years of consistent profitability.

The true market master understands that his/her behavior and understanding is what delivers the profits year after year. The strategy is only the tool they utilize as they take money from the markets. Give a painter a paintbrush, and he will paint you a picture. Give a true artist a piece of chalk, a pencil, or the finest paints money can buy and he will create a thing of beauty. The tools are immaterial; it is the eye and mind that drives them which brings value. Don't allow your mind to get buried under mounds of analysis structure or trading systemology. Work on developing your mind's eye, and you will be able to extract profitability from just about every plausible strategy.

Find an Edge That Fits Your Makeup

With so many profitable trading strategies to choose from, your main task is to find an edge that fits your psychological makeup. On paper, a setup might offer incredible profit potential, but if you can't execute your trade plan without error, your edge remains little more than a theoretical probability.

I find that traders tend to fall into one of two psychological camps. The first has a more nervous, and driven personality. This group is especially vulnerable to whip saws and draw downs, and must constantly defend against emotions. They are prone to becoming manic-depressive in sync with their trading successes/failures. These traders often struggle with deeper–time-frame trading strategies, and produce the most profits when trading high probability/low risk reward ratio trading strategies. Even though I firmly believe that there is lower stress and more profit potential in a high risk reward trading plan, these type "A" traders never seem to be able to position trade effectively. The type "A" trader needs to ring the cash register early and often in order to maintain emotional stability.

I try to steer these traders toward some of the small time-frame market-making and fade strategies that I have developed over the years. The foreign exchange, index futures, and news affected equities tend to be the best vehicles for this psychological profile. These instruments deliver a number of setups each trading day, and are constantly cycling between overbought and oversold levels. Most of the high probability/low risk reward strategies I believe in try to fade a market at its extremes, in the hopes that a reversion to the mean will occur. Therefore, these whipsaw prone instruments offer an excellent trading vehicle for the less patient trader.

Fade Trade

Figure 11.1 shows how a typical fade trade might unfold in the equity markets. ABC Corporation has announced earnings before the bell, and is gapping higher on extraordinary volume. Anytime you see wild volatility expansion married to extreme volume, you know that the crowd is present and is trading a stock. Since the crowd is present, all you have to do is figure out what their directional opinion might be, and position ourselves in the opposite direction in order to make money. If you think about the morning's order flow in a logical manner, you realize that these buy orders are a knee-jerk response to better than expected earnings. As soon as all of the buy side liquidity generated by this news event is satisfied, we can expect the market to implode as it falls through one of our now familiar "air pockets."

Figure 11.1 Example of a fair trade

The fade trader's goal is to capture this small reversion to the mean move. Figure 11.1 shows how the order flow and volume is violent and extreme (1). The odds are extremely high that once an intraday top has been established, the market will have created a large enough air pocket to provide enough profit potential to justify a short biased trade. As you can see, once the buyers were satisfied, the market formed a lower high reversal pattern, and the fade trades setup was complete (2). A short position was established, with protective stop-loss orders set above the reversal pattern's highs. The air pocket that we hoped for did indeed exist, and the price soon collapsed into this illiquid area. It only took 60 minutes before the support offered by the 200-sma was tested, and this acted as an exit signal for the trade (3).

For the type "A" trader, this trade not only produced a profit, but fulfilled her psychological needs at the same time. This fit increases satisfaction when trades work out successfully, and reduces stress and frustration during a payback cycle when losses are being taken. You may argue that this edge is not the most effective for the current market, but since our type "A" trader would likely make emotionally-based trading errors if forced to trade the deeper time frames, this is likely the best possible edge for her portfolio.

While I help the type "A" trader achieve consistent profitability with a trading strategy that fits their psychological profile, I also try to help them develop their inner type "B." While high accuracy/low risk reward ratio trading strategies "feel" comfortable, as you will see in subsequent chapters, I strongly believe they are an inferior and sometimes dangerous way to approach the markets. I believe traders with less intense personalities can be more profitable in the long term. These type "B" traders are more comfortable holding wiggles and giving trends time to mature. I would label myself as a "B" type trader. I am quite comfortable holding a position as it wiggles and jiggles toward my profit objective. I can profitably trade the fast-paced intraday fade trades, but they leave me tired and burnt out by the end of the trading day.

Address the Weekly Price Action

One of my most profitable trading plans is based around weekly price action. These stocks usually deliver an immediate profit after entry; then top out and correct violently. More than half the time they will go well below my break even point before forming a more significant bottom and rallying in earnest.

Most traders cannot comfortably withstand the psychological assault that these trades deliver. To have your account show a 5 percent gain, then a 3 percent loss, then a 15 percent gain can drive many traders to the brink of distraction. I believe it is my personality that allows me to trade these patterns without stress. I know from my research that the risk-to-reward ratios are so rich in these longer-term trend trades, that I am willing to hold them in a *do or die* manner. Some show me a tidy profit, and then decline all the way back to the stop-loss level. However, having analyzed my edge correctly, I know that after taking 20 of these trades over the course of a year, I cannot help but show a strong profit for my efforts. The mathematics of edge is biased so dramatically in my favor that the profit potential of this strategy is well worth any psychological discomfort I may have to endure. Whereas a type "A" trader has a psychological need to be busy, my Nirvana would be a trading strategy that triggers once a month. I could set my computer's alarm systems to alert me when opportunity existed, and ignore the markets the rest of the month.

For traders with patience and a deep–time-frame outlook, I would suggest looking at low accuracy/high risk-to-reward ratio trading strategies. As an example: using multiple–time-frame analysis to enter trades based on an intraday trading setup, yet with a plan to hold the trade for several days based on a daily chart opinion. This type of trading strategy will not yield much in terms of accuracy, but when these trades trend as predicted, the risk-to-reward ratio realized will be astoundingly rich.

Multi–Time-Frame Trend

Figure 11.2 shows a multi–time-frame trend trade that occurred in the Eurodollar versus US dollar currency pair. As you can see from the daily chart below, this market had been trading within the context of a multi-month uptrend. A correction formed after this market topped out near the 1.3700 area. The price pulled back to test the area of support offered by its 20-period exponential moving average (1). As mentioned before, the 20-period exponential moving average is a roving area of support and resistance that many trading constituencies used to trigger the entries and exits of their trading plan. Knowing

Figure 11.2 Example of a multi–time-frame trend trade

that buying pressure was about to hit the market, I dropped down to a small-time-frame intraday chart in the hopes that the market would form a reversal signal with an extremely small risk.

If this were to occur, I knew I could take long exposure with a chance to capture three to five days of rallying action. If the price was able to rally back up to test the highs near €1.3700, I would capture more than 125 pips in profit. I opened a 15 minute chart, and began stalking this currency pairing for an entry. As I began to stalk my trade, the market was sliding lower without any particular hurry or violence (see Figure 11.3). It based near its lows for several hours, then broke down fairly sharply below the €1.3550 level (1). This sell off was obviously the catalyst that the bulls had been waiting for, as a surge of buying spiked the market up quickly over the next 30 minutes. This quick surge of buying soon exhausted itself into an area of chart resistance (2). (Former support once broken becomes resistance when tested.) Minutes after resistance was tested, price collapsed back into the air pocket created by the buying surge.

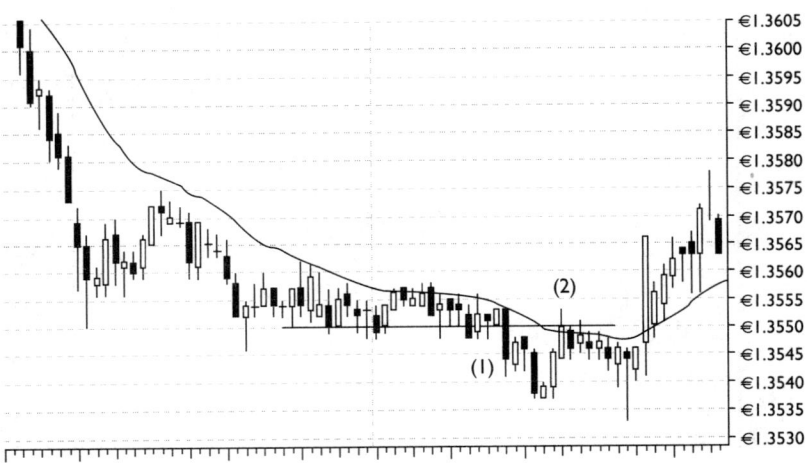

Figure 11.3

This trade gave me my first entry near the €1.3555 level, and I set my stop-loss order below the low at €1.3545. Obviously the trade stopped out for a 10 pip loss, so this series illustrates clearly what I mean by low accuracy/high risk reward trading.

But as luck would have it, the second entry was "the one," and the market reversed this time in earnest. This trade delivered approximately 75 pips of profit before forming a "peek" top, which signaled my exit. With an initial risk of 15 pips, this trade delivered a risk-to-reward ratio of nearly 5 to 1! For every $1,000 I risked, I realized nearly $5,000 in gains. Those are the kind of statistics I want to see on my balance sheet at the end of each month! I cannot stress enough the earning power that large risk-to-reward ratios deliver to your portfolio.

> Over the course of one hundred trades, let us assume your trading strategy delivers 66 losers and 34 winners. If you risk $1,000 on every trade, your account will show gross losses of $66,000 over the course of the one hundred trade sample. However, the 34 winning trades that your strategy delivered produced $2,000 in profit, for gross profits of $68,000. This leaves you with a net gain of $2,000 over the course of 100 trades, and proves that the statistical break even for a 2 to 1 trading strategy lies near 34 percent.

But what if your average risk-to-reward ratio is closer to 3 to 1? Assume that over the course of one hundred trades, your trading strategy delivers 75 losers and 25 winners. If you risk $1,000 on every trade, then your account will show gross losses of $75,000 over the course of the experiment. However, the 25 winning trades that your strategy delivered produce at least $3,000 in profit, or gross profits of $75,000. This leaves you with a net gain of $0 over the course of 100 trades, and proves that a statistical break even for a 3 to 1 trading strategy lies directly at 25 percent. You can see how easy it is to achieve a break-even result, even with an abysmal accuracy rate IF your average risk-to-reward ratio is large enough. Most traders spend an enormous amount of time and effort looking for ways to increase their accuracy, when they would be much better served looking for ways to increase their average risk-to-reward ratio instead.

Large Risk-to-Reward Ratios

It's easy to understand why uninformed traders are so focused on accuracy. It is *satisfying* to be right about a market prediction, and there is an overwhelming bias in the financial media toward hot tips and hot hands. This makes perfect sense when you think about it. The financial media's goal is to keep and attract viewers/listeners/readers. Profitability or return are only selling points, not the primary motivation or reason for existence. As an independent trader it is sometimes easy to forget that the market doesn't care if your predictions come true or not. The mathematics of edge is the sole determinant of profitability. Finding ways to enhance your edge is the only way to increase profitability in the marketplace.

When new students attend one of my seminars, it doesn't matter what country we happen to be in, the majority of them come with the expectation that they will learn not how to make more money, but "how to pick better trades." They are often quite shocked and a bit chagrined when they realize that many of the strategies I am teaching them have low accuracy rates. They feel a bit betrayed at first, but then become quite excited as I convert them to the gospel of large risk-to-reward ratios.

I would be willing to predict that some of you reading this book are feeling slightly skeptical if not downright annoyed by now as you read my statements about accuracy. Let us spend some time working out the mathematics of edge surrounding several different trading strategies, and by the end of this exercise I strongly suspect you to will have changed your thinking about accuracy rates!

Many years ago, when I was still building my skill set as a trader, I started using a stochastic oscillator to trade the equity markets. This indicator was new to me at the time, and I was quite excited at its ability to identify overbought or oversold situations. After several weeks of experimentation, I developed a profitable trading strategy using the oscillator as my primary indicator. Each day I searched the markets for qualifying trades and then waited excitedly for the stochastic to turn higher and thus trigger my entry on the trade. As it stood, the trade was delivering a 48 percent win rate, with an average profit of $1.5 off an initial $1 risk.

Let's analyze the strategy's edge using a 100 trade sample:

$$48 \text{ Winners} \times \$1.5 = \$72 \text{ per share gross profits}$$
$$52 \text{ Losers} \times \$1 = \$52 \text{ per share gross losses}$$
$$\$72 - \$52 = \text{Net gains of } \$20 \text{ per share}$$
$$\$20 \text{ per share} / 100 \text{ trades} = .20 \text{ profit expectation per trade}$$

I traded this strategy quite profitably for a time before I came to a startling realization. When I identified a trade as a qualified candidate, it was consistently 3/8 of a point (37.5 cents per share) lower than the actual trigger/entry level. I started looking at my trade history to see how many qualifying trades failed to reach their trigger point and "set up." I wanted to know how badly my accuracy would suffer if I just entered the trade arbitrarily as soon as I identified it as a qualifying pattern.

This was the first time I had analyzed my edge as a separate entity—as the primary focus rather than simply the derivative of a new trading strategy. This was the point at which my development as an edge analyst began. I marked this experience as one of the major turning points in my development as a trader.

My research indicated that approximately 10 trades out of the last 100 instances failed to trigger. This seemed like an acceptable reduction in accuracy, so I began to analyze how changing my entry strategy would affect my profitability. Remember, not only would I be gaining an additional 3/8 (37.5 cents per share) on my winning trades, but I would also avoid that same 3/8 of a point on every loser! The only downside of this shift in entry strategy would be the fact that 10 of the trades I took out of every hundred would fail to trigger and end up as a loss. I started to calculate the difference in edge between these two entry strategies, and became quite excited at the result! Although I expected my win rate to drop down to 38 percent, these 38 winners would be producing 1 7/8 ($1.875 per share) on average; an increase of 25 percent over my previous average of $1.5 per share. Even more exciting was that the 62 losers I would expect to take would only cost me $.63 apiece instead of the $1 I was used to. Whereas before I had a trade strategy with a 1.5 to 1 risk-to-reward ratio, now I was look-ing at a strategy that would deliver 3 to 1 on my money! (1.875 average profit/.625 average loss = 3 to 1 R/R ratio!)

Let's see how this simple shift in entry strategy would have affected my profitability using the same 100 trade sample:

38 Winners × $1.875 = $71.25 per share gross profits
62 Losers × $.625 = $38.75 per share gross losses
$71.25 − $38.75 = Net gains of $32.50 per share
$32.50 per share / 100 trades = .325 profit expectation per trade

So by simply entering the market when I found a qualifying trade, I would have increased my profit expectations by more than 60 percent! Not only was this new trade management style less time-consuming, but it was eminently more profitable. The only sacrifice I had to make was a psychological one. Every time I took a trade, I knew that there was a 62 percent chance that the trade was going to end up triggering my stop-loss order and cost me money. It was only going to win 38 percent of the time, but the dramatic increase in profitability would act as a soothing salve for any bruising my ego might suffer.

Since I went through this learning experience early in my trading career I assumed that my peers would have also discovered that accuracy is a grossly overrated parameter. You can imagine my surprise when I started my edge consultant practice, and found that the majority of my clients, even those very much on the professional side of market, are constantly seeking accuracy increases rather than focusing on their risk-to-reward ratio.

Accuracy Is Grossly Overrated

Imagine this scenario: A small hedge fund hires me to fly in and take a look at their trading programs in the hope that I could offer them some ideas that would increase their performance. I asked them for statistics on the trades taken in the last quarter, and started by crunching the numbers to determine their basic edge statistics. I soon discovered that this firm, like so many others, was trading a high accuracy/low risk reward strategy. In the last quarter, their trading strategy produced 280 winners, and 113 losers. Their average gain was an abysmal .8 units per trade (for every $1,000 they risked, they only gained $800), but with an accuracy rate near 71 percent, they were consistently profitable.

Their basic edge statistics were as follows:

393 trades were taken in the last quarter.
280 Winners $\times$ .8 units = 224 units gross profits
113 Losers $\times$ 1 = 113 units gross losses
224 − 113 = Net gain of 111 units per quarter
111 Units net profit / 393 trades = .282 unit profit
expectation per trade

I knew that I could help this firm, and began to question them about their trading system. While they couldn't give me many details, they were able to reveal that the trades were based on a set of proprietary indicators which they applied to daily price action. Their practice was to run their algorithm on the markets each day after the close, and enter all qualifying trades the following session using a traditional bar break setup. They would enter the trade when price broke out above the previous day's high, and would set their protected stop-loss levels below that bar's low.

Since so many trading systems trigger their entries/exits around the high or low of the previous session, I was curious to find out how bad their normal levels of slippage were. (Slippage being the difference between the price you wanted to pay, and the fills you actually got.) They were a bit defensive when I asked this question, and I got the feeling that slippage was a bit of a sore point at the firm. This didn't surprise me, because if there ever was a crowd entry point, it is the breakout above the previous day's high, and as we know, the crowd always loses out, therefore buying a breakout above the previous day's high had to be a suboptimal entry point.

Remembering my experience trading stochastics, I asked them to estimate how many times out of a hundred the stocks on their qualified list failed to set up. Anecdotally, they felt that this number would be quite small. I asked them to analyze what the previous quarter's returns would have been had they simply entered every qualified trade at the open. The first five minutes of trading session are extremely liquid, and I felt this would sharply reduce their slippage. In addition, thinking logically, I reasoned that once a trade met their qualifications, there were only three possible outcomes for the following day. One, the market would open flat and then rally up and trigger their buy point above the previous day's high. Two, the stock would open down and never muster the strength needed to trigger. Or three, the stock could gap strongly higher, triggering their entry at the opening tick. In the first two scenarios, an entry at the open would likely be much cheaper than if they waited for the high of the day trigger point. If the market gapped up at the open, then the entry point would be the same for both entry strategies. So the real question was, would the open tick entry make enough money on the winners, and avoid enough loss on the losers in order to offset the inevitable decrease in accuracy?

They asked their accounting department to model the difference between the two entry strategies, and we broke for lunch. Upon returning, we were all delighted with the data that was waiting for us. A market on open entry strategy would have delivered 263 winners, and 130 losers. But in concert with this drop in accuracy (66 percent win rate versus 71 percent) was an explosion in profit potential. The average gain in terms of points didn't grow that significantly, but when compared to the average loss (now slightly smaller due to the market on open entry strategy), their average gain now sported a 1.1 to 1 risk-to-reward ratio!

These changes in outcome would have worked together to deliver the following performance for the trailing quarter.

The same 393 trades were analyzed from the last quarter.
263 Winners × 1.1 units = 289.3 units gross profits
130 Losers × 1 = 130 units gross losses
289.3 − 130 = Net gain of 159.3 units per quarter
159.3 Units net profit / 393 trades = .405 profit
expectation per trade

By changing one small aspect of their trading plan, this firm would have taken in 40 percent more profit in the previous quarter (159 units versus 111). If they had been risking one quarter of 1 percent on each trade, waiting for the market to confirm their entry with a price trigger cost them a whopping 12 percent in the previous quarter. That is an enormous quantity of money to spend on psychological comfort, and in my strong opinion that is exactly what we are doing when we demand confirmation or otherwise hedge our market risks. I strongly believe that the market only offers its profit to those willing to trade "uncomfortable" setups.

A "Safe" Trade Can Blow Up

Every time I take what feels like a "safe" trade, I either make very little, or the trade blows up in my face. Nobody likes losing money, or getting hurt by the market, so naturally the crowd clusters around those trading styles that offer the illusion of safety or comfort. Here are a few examples:

Long-Term Capital Management

One of the clearest examples of this in my mind was the downfall of Long-Term Capital Management. This now legendary hedge fund opened its doors in 1994 with more than $1 billion of investor capital. It was led by some of the best brains in the business, including the former head of bond trading at Salomon Brothers, Ph.D.'s from Harvard and MIT, as well as two gentlemen who shared the 1997 Nobel Prize in economics.

My understanding of their trading strategy was that they invested in bonds spreads which their mathematical modeling systems told them held an arbitrage opportunity. Essentially they bought one type of bond, and shorted another, trying to profit as the difference in the value of these bonds shifted. The profits available in this type of trade are very small, but mathematically they were deemed to be "nearly a sure thing." This represents the ultimate in high accuracy trading. As we know from our previous analysis, any high accuracy trading model will have hidden within it an extremely poor risk-to-reward ratio. This was the case for Long-Term Capital Management; after four years of consistent returns in excess of 30 percent, the fund finally experienced the loss side of its high accuracy/low risk-to-reward ratio model. The firm lost $4.6 billion in less than four months, and quietly faded away.

I have always held this example up as the ultimate example that cute trading ideas don't work in the long term. And let's face it, how much cuter can you get than a bunch of economics professors and Nobel Prize winners telling you they have developed a complex mathematical model that will deliver you an almost guaranteed arbitrage profit? It is no wonder the street funded them with more than $1 billion before they had even opened their doors for business.

Amaranth Advisors

Amaranth Advisors was another large American-based hedge fund that blew up in spectacular style. The head trader on Amaranth's energy desk was a spread trader who had produced enormous profits for the firm during the bull market in natural gas in 2005. In late September 2006, this trader put on a spread trade at eight to one leverage. He was betting that the difference between the March and April futures price for natural gas contracts maturing in the year to come would widen.

It didn't.

Amaranth Advisors lost approximately $6.5 billion *in a single week* as the spread moved violently the wrong way. The failure at Amaranth was the single largest hedge fund collapse in history.

Victor Niederhoffer

Finally, we come to the story of Victor Niederhoffer. This hedge fund manager became well known to the public upon publication of his book *The Education of a Speculator.* Niederhoffer's downfall came (you guessed it) as the result of a high accuracy/low risk reward trading strategy. In 1997, Niederhoffer sold a very large number of put options on the S&P 500 index. Buying a put option gives one the right, but *not the obligation,* to sell his position to the seller of the option at a certain time for a certain price.

Much like a bookie making the line in Vegas for a sporting event, the options markets price the value of options based on the likelihood that the right to execution will be exercised before the time in the option expires. When Niederhoffer sold his put options, the market was in an uptrend and the likelihood that the market would decline far enough for his options to be exercised was infinitesimal. Niederhoffer was placing a trade in which there was a large probability that he could make a small amount of money, but as with any high accuracy/low risk reward trading strategy, his level of leverage was high, and his risk-to-reward ratio was extremely low.

I am sure Niederhoffer had executed the same trading strategy hundreds of times with nothing but positive results over years as a trader. But on October 27, 1997 the market declined 7.7 percent and posted its largest one-day drop in history. In that one horrible session, Niederhoffer lost everything—his hedge fund, his personal savings, his open stock positions. He had to shut down his firm, borrow money and mortgage his house, and sell his quite remarkable silver collection. One cannot possibly comprehend how shocking it would be to have your quite comfortable finances evaporate literally overnight.

These traders all risked enormous quantities of money based on their belief about market direction. They were confident that their analysis was correct, and that the market would move in the direction that would benefit their positions. Contrast that with my personal style of trading. Utilizing a low accuracy/ high risk-to-reward ratio model, my winning trades feel like welcome surprises. When I enter a trade, I do so with full knowledge that the odds are extraordinarily high for the trade to fail and trigger my protective stop-loss order. Since I go into the trade expecting to lose, my main focus is on minimizing my capital loss while maintaining the potential for gain. Because I am expecting to lose on every trade, psychologically the pain of these losses are negligible. I take these losses with a sense of pride, knowing that each opportunity buys me the right to capitalize on a large trend reversal should one occur.

Attractions of the FOREX Market

I recently managed an open position in the Eurodollar. This market showed signs of capitulation (see Figure 11.4), and I took some long exposure in case the intraday bottom I saw forming could turn out to be "the bottom" for this currency pairing (1). It wasn't, and my stop-loss order was soon executed for a 10 pip loss. The next morning a double bottom reversal pattern had formed, and I again added exposure in anticipation of a more serious reversal (2).

Figure 11.4

As luck would have it, this time I won the lottery. I was pleasantly surprised to watch the Euro reverse with a vengeance and begin to accelerate to the upside. As you can see, a double top formed, and I took my profits in reaction to this topping formation (3). I held this position for three days, and each morning fully expected that I would wake up and find that my stop-loss orders were triggered. Instead, I woke up and was pleasantly surprised to find that my open profits had increased during the night! I closed the trade with a little more than 8 to 1 in profits.

Let's do the math to discover the break even point for an eight to one trading strategy if 100 trades are taken:

88 are losers and produce a gross loss of 88 units.
$$88 \times 1 = 88$$
12 are winners and produce a gross profit of 96
$$12 \times 8 = 96$$
Then your net profit is 8
$$96 - 88 = 8$$

With the mathematics of risk reward pushing this much edge behind you, how can you ever be afraid of the market? You don't have to be right very often to make money, and if you are right just once in awhile, you will make a great deal of money. I firmly believe that this style of trading has no inherent risk of implosion. In all my years as a trader, my worst uncontrolled loss came from a stock that gapped against me overnight. I had taken an overnight position based on an intraday reversal, and had placed my stop below an area of support I thought to be particularly important. Some bad news came out overnight, and the stock gapped down radically the following morning.

Because I had a live stop market order resting with my broker, I was filled at the opening tick for a four unit loss. For every $1,000 of risk in the trade, I lost $4,000. So the worst catastrophic loss of my entire career was less than a "nice profit" from one of my 5 to 1 gainers! It only took one or two winning trades to recover from my draw down and move my account equity on to new highs. This is true risk control, and it is why I sleep well at night!

I choose a monthly maximum I'm willing to lose on my Forex trading program. Each month, I add or subtract capital from the account in order to bring it back to my monthly maximum level. This allows me to "go for broke" each month, trading aggressively and without fear as I already know how much money is at risk for the month. Because I'm willing to risk losing the entire account, the percentage returns I achieve each month can be fairly astounding (50 percent – 100 percent monthly returns are not extraordinary). I believe the ability to open a small account, and run it up significantly is one of the main attractions of the Forex market.

When I launched my Forex trading newsletter, I put $1,000 into an account, and banked an average of 10 percent a week for 16 weeks as a publicity stunt. The account peaked out above $7,000, and shows the kind of short-term earning power available to an active speculator.

When I launched my Forex trading newsletter, I put $1,000 into an account, and banked an average of 10 percent a week for 16 weeks as a publicity stunt. The account peaked out above $7,000, and shows the kind of short-term earning power available to an active speculator.

When trying to reach my goal for one of these challenges, I focus on high yielding trend trades with the potential to deliver explosive risk-to-reward ratios. I will take the maximum amount of risk possible on each trade, and will recalculate my position size after each gain or loss. I expect wild account volatility as my low accuracy/high risk-to-reward ratio often produces a series of losers, then one or more explosive gains. Since I'm not sure how large my winners will be, I can't accurately forecast how long any of these challenges may take. If the markets trend well, it might take just a

Insider's Advice   I use this same risk first approach when dealing with performance goals in my trading. I start with the amount of money in terms of absolute dollars or percentage of account value that I'm willing to lose on a particular trading strategy. Normally, this means segregating an account mentally, and having the discipline to cease trading if the risk level that you predetermined is ever reached. When dealing with an equities account, you're often trading an account in which the capital is an important part of your net worth. A much more defensive risk control strategy is required, and therefore the returns on the account as a whole are much smaller. One of the things I love about the foreign exchange markets as a trading instrument is its low capital requirement and ridiculously high leverage. With firms offering 200 or even 300 to 1 leverage, you can literally risk your entire account or any fraction on a given trade.

couple weeks. If the markets are chaotic and choppy, I will not have many setups to trade, and it could take much longer. I really enjoy working through these most entertaining challenges, as they prove in a real-world environment how the tactics contained in this book can be put to use.

CHAPTER 12

HIRING A MONEY MANAGER

Sometimes your best investments are the ones you don't make.

—Donald Trump

Trading is a difficult business; it isn't for everyone. Identifying that this business is a poor fit for your lifestyle, psychology, or family situation is as important as learning to trade well in the first place. If you come to the realization that the money you make trading isn't worth the stress it brings to your life, then don't despair. All of the work you have done to date will allow you to effectively analyze the value of the offerings from the money-management community!

By understanding how money is made in the markets, you are in a very powerful position as firm after management firm contacts you to seek business. It is important to ask the same awkward questions of a would-be money manager as you asked yourself when developing your own trading plan.

Watching how they respond when asked to discuss their risk management strategy will tell you an enormous amount about their experience and market understanding. As discussed previously, the post-millennium era has been one of debacle after debacle for the industries of finance. From the gross accounting irregularities at Enron and WorldCom to the disastrous returns by many widely held mutual funds, or the outright implosions at Long-Term Capital Management and Amaranth Advisors, all have the potential to cripple one's chances for retirement. And remember, when you are dealing with a money manager, more often than not, you are talking about giving him/her the bulk of your true net worth to manage.

So far we have discussed trading primarily within the context of a risk capitalized hobby or business. The money in such an account should be risked with care, but if the account's balance falls to zero, those losses will not materially affect your lifestyle, mortgage payments, or ability to retire. It is critical that you develop a powerful respect for the damage markets can inflict, and only assume the risks that you or your financial advisors deem appropriate for the capital in question. Only a fool would put money into a speculative trading program that he/she cannot afford to lose.

Because a money manager will likely have custody over money you cannot afford to lose, risk management and asset allocation become critical questions as you work to develop your investment plans. The primary goal for any responsible money manager is capital preservation. Therefore, having exposure to a mixture of different asset classes is important as correct asset allocation will work to buffer the volatility of your equity curve. By investing in different asset classes with non-correlated returns, you increase the chances that by the time you're ready to retire, your investment accounts will be large enough for you to live comfortably. If you have traded your own money for any period of time, you know how difficult this business can be.

It should come as no shock for you to learn that only one out of four mutual funds beat the S&P 500 index in a given year. Simply stated, the odds are 75 percent that the mutual funds that you or your financial advisor chose will *underperform* the major market indexes! Since this is the case, why are there more mutual funds available to the investing public than *the individual stocks that make up their holdings?* The answer to that question is found by looking at how the majority of financial planners and retirement advisers are compensated. As usual, the crowd does the most uninformed thing when it comes to investing and ruins their edge in doing so. The average uninformed investor learns that they can trade stocks for a half cent per share, and immediately fires the family stockbroker. What they don't realize is that the $75 commission this professional charges clients doesn't just pay for the trade, it compensates for the skill and experience a broker brings to the market.

The trade at the super discount broker might only cost $3, but what assurances does the investor have that fills will be competitive? A broker with experience will be skilled at order execution, and this can mean a fill $.10 to $.25 better in some illiquid markets. That is a difference of $100-$250 on a 1000 share order. And what about the advice the professional can offer her clients? We know that the crowd always makes the worst possible investment decisions. A broker who is willing to guide clients can save them tens of thousands of dollars by helping them avoid the long entries into periods of euphoria or panic selling into capitulation that are so typical among the majority of investors.

The management fee has also shrunk dramatically in recent years. As fees are reduced, financial planners rely more and more on commissions and bonuses from vendors to earn a living. This conflict of interest has come about due to the ignorance of the crowd. Supply and demand are some of the most powerful forces on the planet; when supply is restricted from one direction, new avenues always open up. We spend much of our adult lives earning a living. After taxes, housing costs, transportation costs, and every other living expense, many have little left over to put into savings. However, the money in your savings account will have as much impact on your quality of life in later years as your health! People will make great efforts to maintain or increase their health, but will hand over hard earned money to a boiler shop operator on little more then a story and a sales script!

Make no mistake the person who helps manage your finances should be as carefully selected as your doctor or lawyer. This person will have a great deal of influence over your investment future. This relationship must be built on trust, experience, and respect. It continually boggles my mind how little effort most investors put into a decision that can affect their lives so deeply.

Questions to Ask Your Financial Advisor

Based on my experience working with successful traders and managers, there are five questions that need to be answered to your satisfaction before anyone gains the privilege of managing your assets.

1. How Do You Control Your Risk in Each Position?

Risk control is the number one factor that determines consistent performance. Before any investment is made, a competent money manager will already have considered the downside potential, and will have created an exit plan in case the investment goes sour. In a market that has produced 50 percent, 70 percent, even 90 percent losses in individual equities, controlling the damage from your losers is the only way to keep your head above water.

An investor should *never* take a 50 percent loss on her money. Having a proper risk control plan in place will ensure that the stock is sold before the damage can reach these disastrous levels.

Another question that is import to ask is whether or not risk is consistent across all the open positions. It is vital for any market participant to keep losses and gains in balance with one another. It is a recipe for disaster to lose $3,000 on one position and make $1,000 on another. Losses are part of this business; the question is not if they will occur, but how will losses be offset by gains in the portfolio. You want a money manager to be able to tell you what tactics they would choose to balance your risk across all open positions.

2. How Do You Convert Paper Profits Into Real Gains?

How many times have you seen an investment rally provide you with a large paper profit, then collapse rapidly as you watch your paper profits vanish? The market cycles constantly between overbought and oversold, undervalued and overvalued, cheap and dear. Remember, as a rally creates profits for you, it creates profits for many other market participants as well. When they believe the stock is fully valued, they will begin to take their profits. In many cases, this selling pressure may be more than the stock can bear. Just as the money manager must have a plan in place in case the investment slips, so should they have a plan in effect to determine how to manage a successful outcome. An appropriate price target should be set, and when the price reaches this level profits should be realized.

While you may not understand the minutia of her trading plan, you should be able to get a sense of her mastery on the subject. To be a successful manager, a trading plan is the nearest and dearest thing to one's heart. Discussing its philosophy and fundamental construction should not be a uncomfortable subject.

3. What Is the Average Draw Down One Might Expect to Experience?

Return is always a factor of risk assumed. The more risk you assume, the higher your returns will be if you're successful and the larger your losses will be if unsuccessful. Looking at the draw downs or losing streaks a money manager has experienced in the past will allow you to gain insight into how much risk this manager takes. If you deposit $10,000, and your account grows to $20,000 at the end of the year, that is all well and good. But what if during that year your account fell to $5,000 on its way to $20,000? Would that amount of account volatility be acceptable to you? Some managers take excessive risk in order to be able to post big numbers for marketing purposes when they do well. Your money deserves better, so look for a manager who has kept draw downs small and controlled during her career. Consistency breeds consistency, and good trading is very boring; it is best in my experience to seek out a person with a "slow and steady wins the race" management style.

4. Are You Performance Compensated?

Like a lawyer working on contingency, you want your money manager to have a vested interest in your money's growth. If your manager works directly for you, then this question is easily answered. If he works for a firm, find out if his compensation (bonus) is based on management fees and bonuses tied to client account performance, or if it is based on mutual fund commissions, firm fees generated, or new accounts opened. You want to be working with someone who has a personal investment in your success. A fairly large management fee may seem expensive in the beginning, but in the end your returns will likely be far better if there is a profit incentive for the manager. As long as the customer remains the manager's largest revenue source, you're likely to have a long and profitable relationship.

5. How Do You Feel About Being Entirely in Cash?

A wise trader once said: "There is a time to be bullish, a time to be bearish, and a time to be fishing!" A good money manager will understand the power of nonparticipation, and will be willing to stand aside when the market offers little opportunity. Think how dramatically a money manager would have outperformed the majority of mutual funds by simply remaining in cash for the majority of 2002! Look for a money manager who has the guts to be flat when it's appropriate!

Make the effort to have these five questions answered to your satisfaction by anyone you are considering for a money management relationship. By covering these issues up front, you will dramatically increase your chances for a positive and profitable experience with those whom you entrust with your money.

Consider Your Investment Philosophy

I have written before about my distaste for "cuteness" when it comes to investment philosophy. Please keep this in mind if presented with a new "can't miss" investment opportunity. Remember how perfect Long-Term Capital Management's pitch would have sounded on paper, and how badly it ended for investors. Read all prospectuses and analyze their trading concepts with your new found edge analysis skills, and only invest with entities that you feel focus on finding the best risks the market offers. In my strong opinion, you should avoid any investment pitches that are heavily focused on hedging, spreading, or strategies that otherwise seek to avoid losses. As I hope you now realize, small losses are to be embraced as the entry fee needed to have the right to participate in a significant trend.

If a fund is particularly "hot," try to determine why. If good performance has attracted the crowd's attention to a new or perhaps niche market based fund, it is entirely possible that the massive influx of new funds is creating an artificial demand imbalance in the fund's major holdings. As the money streams in, the fund managers have a fiduciary responsibility to put it to work. Every day they buy more shares, and in the short term, drive up their own performance numbers. But sooner or later, euphoria will occur, and suddenly their stocks will implode as the air pocket created by a sustained surge of buying works itself out. Usually these implosion periods will occur like clockwork just after a product builds support and there is widespread media exposure (i.e., as soon as the crowd discovers it). Surprised? You shouldn't be. By now you should have a level of market understanding which will keep you from being part of the crowd for the rest of your life!

Investing With ETFs

Since mutual funds rarely beat the indexes, and have management fees that can run a couple of percentage points, why use them? In the beginning, mutual funds offered individual investors the ability to take broadly diversified exposure to a market with a very small investment. These days, individual investors can achieve the same goals with a great deal more control at a fraction of the cost by putting their capital into Exchange Traded Funds or ETFs. An ETF is an exchange traded security that tracks or replicates the performance of a major stock market index, market sector, or commodity. These funds are bought and sold on the stock exchanges, with the same order mechanics and commissions as any individual equity. Since they act as proxies for their tracking vehicle, there is a profit opportunity for the arbitrage community anytime an ETF moves away from the price of the instrument it tracks. Complex computer programs watch for minute discrepancies and will flood the ETF with capital until the profit opportunity vanishes as it comes back into alignment. Because of this profit incentive, these ETFs track the instrument they were designed to follow with near perfect precision.

Because these funds are proxies for an index, country, or sector, they are mechanically and rigidly managed. This makes the management process an almost entirely clerical one, and as a result, the management fees for these funds charge are remarkably small. For example, the "spyders" ETF replicates the price action of the S&P 500 index, and has an expense ratio of 0.08 percent. There are exchange traded funds that track every index and sector under the sun; exchange traded funds that offer exposure to the major market indexes in Japan, Austria, Belgium, France, Germany, Spain, South Africa, Brazil, China, Malaysia, and on and on! The incredible choice and extraordinary liquidity exchange traded funds offer make them my favorite tool for longer-term investments when retirement account type capital is at stake. For links to sites with educational information, and lists of available exchange traded funds, please visit my homepage at www.boyoder.com.

Many money managers or financial advisors don't utilize exchange traded funds because there is no commission for them. This is yet another reason why you need to be sure that your money manager is being paid by you, not some third party. There is no free lunch, especially in the financial services industry. Follow the money and you will soon have the information to decide if you are being well served by your current asset manager.

The upsell is another grand tradition within the financial industry. One product or service is offered at cost, or perhaps a slight loss, in order to attract the customer. This low rate of return is compensated by high fee products and services sold to the client at a later date. As usual, it is crowd behavior to get suckered into a free deal, and the likelihood is high that they will end up paying more in the end. In life, it pays to be frugal. The dollar saved is truly the dollar earned. But in keeping with the perverse nature of trading, the financial industry rewards frugality with underperformance and lost opportunity. It always amazes me when I speak at one of the industry conventions, how attendees will go to extraordinary lengths to try to haggle some small discount for instructional services, then go back home and hemorrhage $5,000 into the market because of their lack of education and experience.

Sometimes...Its Just a Simple Shift in Strategy

The trading game is one built on ideas and concepts. I purchased a $50 book that gave me one idea that is now developed into a trade worth thousands of dollars per month. It only takes one or two concepts or breakthroughs to radically affect one's profitability. Just look back at the examples from my experience with stochastics. A simple shift in entry strategy can produce an enormous increase in average gain.

One gentleman engaged me to help him improve his intraday trading plan. He had failed to show a profit for the last three months, and was unable to account for his failure. We spent several hours analyzing his strategy, and I came to believe that his underperformance was due to emotional trading errors, rather than weakness in his trading plan. I offered some suggestions on how he might work to reduce stress and increase his trading discipline. We spoke regularly over the next couple of weeks, and he did splendidly with my support and reminders about which behavior was correct according to his trading plan.

Then a payback cycle began. I was excited to be working with him, because it was during these periods of loss that he gave back all his profits and then some. If I could teach him how to identify payback and reduce his risk and aggressiveness during this time, I felt sure his month to month profitability would return. Yet after one unprofitable week, he canceled our appointments citing the expense of regular consulting sessions.

Less than a month later he was back, having lost close to $20,000 during the payback cycle. By trying to save $500, he ended up losing $20,000. We had a built in circuit breaker in the plan we developed that would put him in cash and halt trading for a week if a draw down reached the $10,000 level. I know if we had continued working together during the draw down, he would have stuck to his plan and proper behavior would have saved him at least $10,000.

Another client had been trading for some time, but had been intrigued by a presentation he saw me give at one of the industry gatherings. We worked together on one specific strategy, and at the end of the month had developed an extremely robust trading plan to exploit this edge with maximum efficiency. Our task finished, he thanked me, and said goodbye. I met with him some six months later at another event, and he offered to buy me a drink. We chatted for a while, talked about the markets and trading in general. When the cocktails arrived, he proposed a toast to the trade plan we had developed. He told me that strategy had delivered him more than $100,000 in gains the first month he traded it!

Pay attention to the earning power that the markets can deliver with the addition of just one new idea or concept. When you are analyzing the offerings of the financial services industry, remember that there is no free lunch. I would be willing to guarantee that if an offer seems too good to be true, it without a doubt is! Nobody wants a cheap brain surgeon, or a deep discount face lift. With the ability to affect your financial future at such a high level, you cannot afford a cheap money manager! You get what you pay for; you owe it to yourself to buy quality where your financial future is concerned.

Reward Is Correlated to Risk

A good money manager will not only manage your risk, but will help you develop appropriate expectations for performance. Reward is always directly correlated to risk. The more market risk you are willing to accept, the higher your expected rate of return will be. Predicting profits for the year is a difficult task for the investment-focused money manager. The greater the trade frequency, the better your accuracy will be at predicting an appropriate profit expectation. The mathematics of risk-to-reward still dictates the final outcome for investment time-frame trades, but these positions are much more dependent on the markets trend. Month-to-month, even quarter-to-quarter, your gains will be randomly mixed. With the deepest time-frame trades, the bulk of the year's profits are often made in just a few weeks of dramatic movement. Trading price action at a weekly, monthly, or quarterly level is definitely a "be right and sit tight" endeavor.

My experience working with professionals in the finance industry leads me to believe that an enormous amount of edge is left behind by traders trying to tailor their trading program's equity curve to the tastes of the uninformed public. Very few members of the investing public understand that the big money—the real wealth creation—comes from "the long pull." Active trading brings in a steady stream of income, but carries with it an enormous amount of overhead in terms of commissions, fees, and time spent working. This is fine if your trading is a business, and you need the consistency of income.

An investor however might have a retirement goal set 20 years into the future. Month-to-month profitability should be the last thing on his mind. Just as there is an inversely proportional ratio between accuracy and average risk-to-reward ratio, I strongly believe there is a steep price to be paid for month-to-month consistency. Again and again in my career, I have been positioned perfectly to capture extraordinary trends, but have missed out on those gains because I had rung the cash register on a smaller–time-frame trade. I remember one trade taken in the stock of Yahoo during the Internet bubble era. I saw an intraday reversal, and initiated my position with a 3 to 1 profit expectation. The stock soon rallied to meet my goal. I took my profits and moved on to the next trade. Over the course of the next week, the stock exploded to the upside. It printed a rally of 100 points, the profits from which would have more than doubled my income for the year. However, this rally was a complete shock to me, I did not see it coming, and did not have any plan in place to capture such a move.

Insider's Advice   With an average risk-to-reward ratio coming in around 5 to 1, there are always one or two trades that absolutely explode and offer me 15–25 to 1! These windfall gains will make a decent year great, and a good year into one of fantastic returns. If you expect your money manager to produce each and every month, then know that you are limiting your upside in an account where time is on your side. Instead, rate your manager's performance on a quarterly or yearly basis against the performance goals and risk levels established at the outset of the relationship.

I executed my trading plan without error, and did correctly predict the price action within its parameters. Therefore, I couldn't really beat myself up for missing out on the 100 point move. It was never part of my trading plan, so therefore I didn't deserve to participate in the rally. The goal of my trading program was to make the money I need to buy food, clothing, and shelter for the month. Wealth generation was a secondary motivation. Because of the pressures of trading for a living, I knowingly and willingly sacrificed the unknown upside potential in my trades, in order to ensure myself the best possible chance at a profit for the month.

In another account, my goals are very different. This is money for the future. Unless I experience a personal disaster in which I need immediate funds, these monies are to be compounded until I need them in retirement years. Unlike my income generating trading programs, which generate a trade four to eight times a week, I primarily position trade these funds. When I feel an ETF or individual equity is about to experience a major trend change, I take my risk and wait for the trend to mature until euphoria is reached.

CHAPTER 13

PUTTING IT ALL TOGETHER

There is a theory which states that if ever for any reason anyone discovers what exactly the universe is for and why it is here, it will instantly disappear and be replaced by something even more bizarre and inexplicable. There is another theory that states that this has already happened.

—DOUGLAS ADAMS

By now I hope you have already begun experimenting with some of the ideas presented. Whether you interact with the markets for fun, to put food on the table, or are just interested in using this knowledge to find the best manager to invest your capital, you are entering a world that offers incredible freedom and income potential. I hope my arguments have convinced you of the validity of my views. My experiences as a trader, speaker, writer, and analyst have helped me to form very strong opinions about market principles and behaviors. Socrates once said,

Employ your time improving yourself by other men's writings, so that you may gain easily what others have labored hard for.

I have learned a great deal from others in my industry, and hope now that some of you may find value in these pages. For those of you in the beginning stages of your trading career, welcome! As a trader, you are given a unique chance to create your own reality. By deciding which instrument, time frame, trading style, and strategy to exploit, you can work your trading around just about any lifestyle. Own the markets, never let them own you! Far too many traders let the market dictate a reality to them, and are enslaved to its wiggles and jiggles evermore. Since I hope you now believe along with me that the crowd is always wrong, spend a good deal of time thinking about what makes you different, why you will be able to profit where so many other market participants will fail. There is a great deal of room for individuality and creativity in this business as long as you remember a few unalterable truths.

- *You are trading with a set of statistical probabilities. It is impossible to know which trades will win, which trades will lose.*
- *You can only capture the profits the market makes available to your edge.*
- *Bigger size equals bigger income. More markets, more positions, more strategies will tend to reduce income.*
- *You must take more money from the markets on your winning trades than you give back on your losers.*

By developing your own edges, and creating a trading plan around them, you will detach yourself from the crowd and their unprofitable behaviors. As you become more comfortable living outside the envelope of conventional wisdom, your lapses of objectivity and emotional trading errors will dry up and fade away. You will begin to see the price action on your chart as a storyboard telling the tale of order flow and market emotion. The markets will cease to be battlegrounds where sacrifice and pain lead to conquest and victory, but rather playgrounds of opportunity where inquisitive experimentation and creative problem solving lead to wealth and personal freedom. When the financial media is talking monolithically about the strength and power of a certain asset class, you will see the signs of euphoria from which you will take your profits and begin capturing profits from the short side of the market. Freeing your mind so that it may "see" what the crowd is doing is based on acceptance. You must accept the risk to capital and to your ego if the trade fails and you are proven wrong. You must believe absolutely that each trade is nothing more than a tiny piece of a very large puzzle, that no one trade alone can make or break you, and there is no personal failure attached to the execution of a stop-loss.

The fear of failure provokes so many strong emotions, and is at the root of many emotional trading errors. When I have a room full of students in front of me at a seminar, I will often pull someone out of the audience and offer them the chance to take a risk based on a coin flip. If there is only a quarter at stake, they flip quickly and easily with a relaxed posture and stress free body language. If I repeat the exercise but raise the stakes to $100, they take their time, their shoulders stiffen, and their body language shows signs of tension and stress. I have changed nothing but the size of the game; the odds are still 50 percent that they will win. But $100 is enough money for them to care about, and so they feel personally invested in the result of the coin flip. Even though they have no control over the outcome, they know that they will feel a sense of failure if they lose.

Capturing the carefree nonchalance of the flip for a quarter is critical for successful trading. If you have dreams to one day make many millions from your trading, then you must get used to winning or losing six figures every day without losing your nonchalance. In my experience, no one can put more pressure on you than yourself, and it is this internal pressure a speculator must overcome in order to thrive.

Run everything you read about trading through a filter of skepticism—this book emphatically included! I have given you ideas to think about, now it is your job to decide if you agree with my concepts. Trust, then verify what you have learned, and you will build strength of faith in your edge and trading plan that few will be able to match. We have all seen the bumper sticker that reads "Question Authority." My version would be "Question Everything." This is especially the case for any consumer of trading education. When I work with my consulting clients, I offer them ideas, concepts, and theories. Then I try to give them a structure with which they may prove those concepts to themselves.

I know that I can accelerate the learning curve for any trader, but in order for the information I offer to have any real impact, each trader must prove its validity to himself. One nice thing about the markets is that they offer absolute proof for theories once research is applied. If I have done the work for you, and am offering you ideas about an edge, then independently verifying the validity of my statements is an easy task.

GOOD LUCK AND GOOD TRADING!

It is literally true that millions come easier to a trader after he knows how to trade than hundreds did in the days of his ignorance.

— JESSE LIVERMORE

T rading is one of the most incredible and unusual businesses on the planet. You can take money from the markets any place on the globe where basic electronic connectivity is present. You can develop a trading style to take money from the markets in a manner that is conducive to your lifestyle *and* your timetable. It is a business that can produce 6, 7, 8 and now even a few 10 figure incomes for people whose names and faces you would probably never recognize. There are almost no startup fees, and if you decide to quit the business, a simple phone call to your broker will put a check for the full amount in the mail.

With all of the wonderfully positive things that trading knowledge can deliver, sometimes these benefits come at great cost. I hope some of the ideas from this book will help you accelerate your learning curve and find a place of balance and harmony in which trading serves *you*, not the other way around.

On one hand, trading is all about numbers and money, but ironically those who focus only on making money rarely succeed! The traders who focus on process, analysis, and who never lose a sense of playful experimentation in their relationship with the markets are the ones who can make money. Their profits are the *byproduct* of their skills, experience, and correct trading behavior. As long as they focus on their process, the mathematics of edge will take care of the rest.

You are very lucky to be trading in the post-millennium era. Never before has such dramatic access to the world's markets been available to any person on the planet. Your hardest task in the years to come will be choosing which instruments to trade! As services surrounding the financial markets continue to commoditize, your trading business overhead will continue to shrink. New edges and trading strategies will become more economically viable, and new disciplines and trading modalities will spring up where none existed before.

Unleash your creative mind, and focus it on objective pattern recognition. Who knows what new patterns, tendencies, or predictive tools you will develop in the years to come! Then, armed with the knowledge I've offered in this book, you should be well informed and well-positioned to reap the maximum reward your discovery makes available!

* * * * *

A quick search on the Internet or a visit to my Web site (www.boyoder.com) will let you know where my next public event will be. I look forward to meeting you and hearing your stories about your learning curve—how you made your breakthroughs and how you have applied your new edge analysis to increase your income as a trader!

There is a great wide world out there just swimming in a sea of capital. Get out there and start taking your share! Good Luck and Good Trading!

BASIC EDGE ANALYSIS WORKSHEET

This worksheet is useful for the beginning stages of edge analysis. As you develop a new trading idea, this worksheet will help you track its profitability, as well as offering you a visual guide to the size and rhythm of its payout/payback cycles.

Simply photocopy the blank sheet and fill in by hand. You can also download the spreadsheet file from www.boyoder.com and log your trades right from your own desktop.

To complete this sheet, fill in each winner or loser in the appropriate columns as they appear. Leave a blank space in the opposite column so that payout/payback cycles can be readily seen. Once you're finished, you will be in a position to calculate all the totals from the upper data box. Keep a running total of the trade's profit and loss in the third column. This will give you a quick glimpse into the draw down cycles of the trade. If working from the electronic version, I suggest setting up a simple line chart of the Running P/L column in the blank space provided to the right of the main data fields.

Following is an example of a completed sheet with the data from the first high risk-to-reward ratio example in Chapter 1.

Bo Yoder's
Basic Edge Analysis Worksheet
www.boyoder.com

Total Trades	# of Winners	# of Losers	P&L
20	4	16	$6,000

	Average Commission	Per Trade Expectation	
	$15	$285	

Average Gain	Average Loss	Average R/R Ratio
$5,500	-$1,000	5.5 to 1

Winners	Losers	Running P&L
	-$1,000	-$1,000
$5,000		$4,000
	-$1,000	$3,000
$5,000		$8,000
	-$1,000	$7,000
	-$1,000	$6,000
	-$1,000	$5,000
	-$1,000	$4,000
	-$1,000	$3,000
	-$1,000	$2,000
	-$1,000	$1,000
	-$1,000	$0
	-$1,000	-$1,000
	-$1,000	-$2,000
$7,000		$5,000
	-$1,000	$4,000
	-$1,000	$3,000
	-$1,000	$2,000
	-$1,000	$1,000
$5,000		$6,000

Copyright 2007 Bo Yoder-Free for personal use.

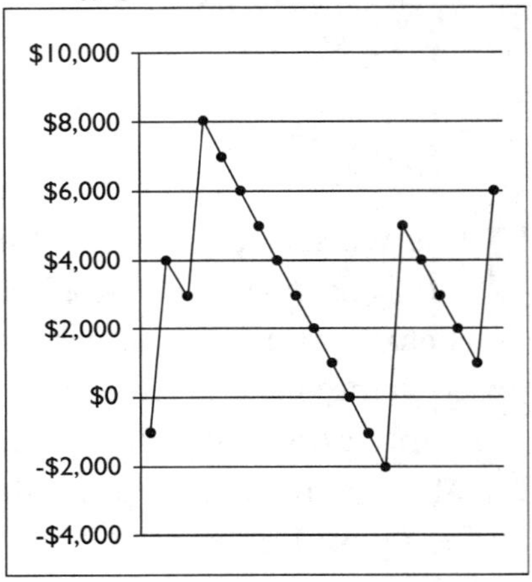

Figure A.1

Bo Yoder's
Basic Edge Analysis Worksheet
www.boyoder.com

Total Trades		# of Winners		# of Losers		P&L
		Average Commission		Per Trade Expectation		
Average Gain		Average Loss			Average R/R Ratio	

Winners   **Losers**   **Running P&L**

Figure A.2

TRADE PLAN WORKSHEET

As I've mentioned again and again, your trade plan is one of the most important aspects of a successful trading program. Your trading plan will act as a behavioral crutch upon which you may lean when the markets go against you or when your emotions run high for reasons external to the market. Spend a good deal of time thinking creatively and philosophically. Use these questions as the basis for your self-evaluation.

1. Describe and define your edge.
2. What are the setups?
3. What market behaviors will you use to develop your market bias?
4. How will the market be required to act in order to trigger your buy and sell signals?
5. What tactics and/or order types will you use to enter and exit your trades?
6. What rules will you use to determine where stop-loss orders shall be set?
7. What tools, methods, and strategies will be used in order to find these setups?

8. Will you trade the strategy in only one time frame? If so, which time frame, and why is it deemed to be the best for this strategy?
9. Is this a strategy that you will trade to the short side as well as the long?
10. What are your strategies for taking profits?
11. What keystone events will you use to determine when you are in the transition zone from *payout to payback?*
12. What keystone events will you use to determine when you are in the transition zone from *payback to payout?*
13. What changes will you make to your position management strategy after you have identified that you are trading within the *context of a payout cycle?*
14. What changes will you make to your position management strategy after you have identified that you are trading within the *context of a payback cycle?*
15. How much money are you willing to lose during the course of a normal draw down before you stop trading and re-examine your edge?
16. How much money are you willing to lose in a month before you stop trading and re-examine your edge?
17. Define what types of setup failure you might see that would make you consider abandoning this strategy?

Once you've taken the time to answer all these questions fully, you are in a position to begin trading your new edge with confidence! By "scrimmaging" with the market during your strategy development process, you will develop a trading plan that covers all the bases. You'll know with precision exactly what actions need to be taken when the market is going in your favor, or more importantly, when it is headed in the wrong direction.

TRADING CHALLENGE WORKSHEET

While this worksheet can be worked out by hand, it is so much more convenient when done on the computer. I suggest downloading the spreadsheet file from www.boyoder.com and following along with the examples below.

The "Target Goal," "Goal Per Week," and "Margin Required" fields should be self-explanatory. The field labeled "Attack Level" controls how close you will go to the maximum number of available contracts for your account size. The contract size for this worksheet is denoted in $100,000 blocks. Therefore .3 contracts would imply a $30,000 position.

Although this worksheet is designed for the foreign exchange market, it can be easily adapted to any contract based trading instrument. Just change the "Margin Required" box to the proper margin level per contract (instead of per $100,000). You will then need to adjust the formula in the P/L column by changing the 10 (profit or loss in dollars per tick) to whatever the point value is for the contract you wish to trade. (If you are trading the S&P E-Mini, you would set this value to 50.)

In the first example, I have filled out the parameters for a $500-to-$20,000 challenge. As you can see, if I can bring in a minimum of 40 pips per week, then I should be able to reach my goals within a couple of months. Note that the "Attack Level" parameter is set at 100 percent for this challenge. This is a "go for broke" setting. Any streak of sustained bad luck will surely blow out the account, and therefore the setting is only appropriate for the most extreme challenges.

In this second example, we see a much more realistic Attack Level. At a 25 percent Attack Level, you are only taking one quarter of the contracts available for your account size. While blowing out the account during an extreme draw down is certainly possible, it would take an enormous run of bad luck, or some serious trade mismanagement to lose all of your money.

Bo Yoder's
Trading Challenge Worksheet
www.boyoder.com

Target Goal		Goal Per Week	Margin required ($100,000)
$20,000		40	$1,350
		Attack Level	
		100%	

Time	Account$$	Pips P/L	Max Size	Contracts	$$P/L
Week 1	500.00	40	0.4	0.3	120
Week 2	620.00	40	0.5	0.4	160
Week 3	780.00	40	0.6	0.5	200
Week 4	980.00	40	0.7	0.7	280
Week 5	1,260.00	40	0.9	0.9	360
Week 6	1,620.00	40	1.2	1.2	480
Week 7	2,100.00	40	1.6	1.5	600
Week 8	2,700.00	40	2.0	2.0	800
Week 9	3,500.00	40	2..6	2.5	1,000
Week 10	4,500.00	40	3.3	3.3	1,320
Week 11	5,820.00	40	4.3	4.3	1,720
Week 12	7,540.00	40	5.6	5.5	2,200
Week 13	9,740.00	40	7.2	7.2	2,880
Week 14	12,620.00	40	9.3	9.3	3,720
Week 15	16,340.00	40	12.1	12.1	4,840
Week 16	21,180.00	40	15.7	15.6	6,240

Table C.1

**Bo Yoder's
Trading Challenge Worksheet
www.boyoder.com**

Target Goal	Goal Per Day	Margin required ($100,000)
$15,000	9	$1,350

**Attack Level
25%**

Copyright 2007 Bo Yoder - Free for personal use.

Time	Account $$	Pips P/L	Max Size	Contracts	$$ P/L
Day 1	25,000.00	9	18.5	4.6	414
Day 2	25,414.00	9	18.8	4.7	423
Day 3	25,837.00	9	19.1	4.7	423
Day 4	26,260.00	9	19.5	4.8	432
Day 5	26,692.00	9	19.8	4.9	441
Day 6	27,133.00	9	20.1	5.0	450
Day 7	27,583.00	9	20.4	5.1	459
Day 8	28,042.00	9	20.8	5.1	459
Day 9	28,501.00	9	21.1	5.2	468
Day 10	28,969.00	9	21.5	5.3	477
Day 11	29,446.00	9	21.8	5.4	486
Day 12	29,932.00	9	22.2	5.5	495
Day 13	30,427.00	9	22.5	5.6	504
Day 14	30,931.00	9	22.9	5.7	513
Day 15	31,444.00	9	23.3	5.8	522
Day 16	31,966.00	9	23.7	5.9	531
Day 17	32,497.00	9	24.1	6.0	540
Day 18	33,037.00	9	24.5	6.1	549
Day 19	33,586.00	9	24.9	6.2	558
Day 20	34,144.00	9	25.3	6.3	567
Day 21	34,711.00	9	25.7	6.4	576
Day 22	35,287.00	9	26.1	6.5	585
Day 23	35,872.00	9	26.6	6.6	594
Day 24	36,466.00	9	27.0	6.7	603
Day 25	37,069.00	9	27.5	6.8	612
Day 26	37,681.00	9	27.9	6.9	621
Day 27	38,302.00	9	28.4	7.0	630
Day 28	38,932.00	9	28.8	7.2	648
Day 29	39,580.00	9	29.3	7.3	657
Day 30	40,237.00	9	29.8	7.4	666

Table C.2

Table C.2 more closely mirrors my personal trading style. I like to know what my needs are in order to reach a particular goal for the month. If I hope to bring in $15,000 from my foreign exchange trading, the spreadsheet tells me that I will need

Bo Yoder's
Trading Challenge Worksheet
www.boyoder.com

Target Goal	Goal Per Week	Margin required ($100,000)
	Attack Level	

Copyright 2007 Bo Yoder - Free for personal use.

Time	Account $$	Pips P/L	Max Size Contracts	$$P/L

Table C.3

to average 9 pips a day in order to meet my monthly goal. Some months your trading will run rich, some months it will be lean, but it gives me a high degree of confidence to know that I can reach my goal without using excessive leverage if I can just maintain an average of so many pips per day. At the end of the month, I withdraw my gains, and begin the process all over again.

PROFIT COMPOUNDING WORKSHEET

This worksheet is intended to help you keep track of your profit reinvestment plan, and is intended for the trader who is focused on a regular income production. While the *Bo Yoder's Trading Challenge Worksheet* showed the extreme power of leveraged compounding, it assumes that one never enjoys the fruits of one's labors until the challenge has reached a successful conclusion. In the real world, there are constant living expenses to take care of. This is why I urge clients in my consulting practice to stick with their day job until they have proven themselves first, and during this time enjoy the luxury of compounding their trading returns 100 percent. If their "regular job" pays their bills, they are in the position to leverage their newfound skills in a maximally efficient manner.

As you saw from the trade challenge examples, extraordinary gains can be realized in a relatively short period of time, if you are willing to take big risks and compound 100 percent. However, it is only responsible to do so when you are trading pure risk capital, and have other forms of income that will cover your living expenses in full.

Once you have the capital needed, and the skills you can rely on to put food on the table as a professional trader, then you are ready to begin using the *Profit Compounding Worksheet* at the end of this appendix. Begin by carefully analyzing your month-to-month budget for living expenses. Add in all recurring bills that have to deal with the necessities of food, clothing, and shelter. Take this number and add on a percentage for cushion, and you have your expected "salary" as a serious trader. This is the money that you will draw out of your trading account each and every month on payday. It doesn't matter whether your returns that month were small or large, whether you posted a gain or a loss. The bills will still come due, and you will spend your "nut" each month whether you like it or not.

This worksheet is set up to track your account on a monthly timescale. Input the size of your "Monthly Nut" in the space provided, and then input the size of your account and that month's profit or loss. (P/L). This is another worksheet that works best on a computer, but if you wish, it can be worked out by hand. There is something to be said for doing everything in long hand. It forces you to deal with the numbers in a conscious manner, and reinforces the reality of your current financial position.

It is said that once a year the great speculator of the 1920s, Jesse Livermore, would order his entire trading account to be liquidated into cash. He would then pack some sandwiches and order himself to be locked in the vault with his money overnight. Surrounded by stacks and stacks of currency, he would work through the night on his trade plan for the coming year. He went through this exercise to remind himself that there was real money, in fact, quite large sums of money, at stake in the year to come.

Having input your monthly nut, account value, and monthly P/L, the spreadsheet will calculate

1. Your percentage return for the month, if your profits exceeded your monthly nut, and if so by how much. This becomes the sum of money that you will leave in your trading account, thus increasing your buying power and expected earnings in the months to come.
2. The risk levels of 1 percent, 2 percent, 3 percent, and 5 percent risk in dollar terms. This offers you a handy guide to position sizing as your trading capital grows little by little during the compounding process.

Here is an example page from the worksheet showing a typical trader's layout.

Bo Yoder's
Profit Compounding Worksheet
www.boyoder.com

	What Is Your **Monthly Nut?** **$10,000**	

Date	Account	Monthly P/L	%Return	Compound $$	1% Risk	2% Risk	3% Risk	5% Risk
Jan-06	$285,750	$15,500	5.42	$5,500	$2,858	$5,715	$8,573	$14,288
Feb-06	$291,250	$9,500	3.26	$0	$2,913	$5,825	$8,738	$14,563
Mar-06	$290,750	$12,375	4.26	$2,375	$2,908	$5,815	$8,723	$14,538
Apr-06	$293,125	-$5,000	-1.71	$0	$2,931	$5,863	$8,794	$14,656
May-06	$278,125	$12,000	4.31	$2,000	$2,781	$5,563	$8,344	$13,906
Jun-06	$280,125	$9,000	3.21	$0	$2,801	$5,603	$8,404	$14,906
Jul-06	$280,125	$3,950	1.41	$0	$2,801	$5,603	$8,404	$14,006
Aug-06	$274,075	$14,000	5.11	$4,000	$2,741	$5,482	$8,222	$13,704
Sep-06	$278,075	$19,250	6.92	$9,250	$2,781	$5,562	$8,342	$13,904
Oct-06	$287,325	$9,875	3.44	$0	$2,873	$5,747	$8,620	$14,366
Nov-06	$287,200	$22,500	7.83	$12,500	$2,872	$5,744	$8,616	$14,360
Dec-06	$299,700	$38,000	12.68	$28,000	$2,997	$5,994	$8,991	$14,985
Jan-07	$327,700	$7,000	2.14	$0	$3,277	$6,554	$9,831	$16,385
Feb-07	$327,700	$4,500	1.37	$0	$3,277	$6,554	$9,831	$16,385
Mar-07	$327,700	-$9,000	-2.75	$0	$3,277	$6,554	$9,831	$16,385
Apr-07	$308,700	$13,000	4.21	$3,000	$3,087	$6,174	$9,261	$15,435
May-07	$311,700	$15,000	4.81	$5,000	$3,117	$6,234	$9,351	$15,585
Jun-07	$316,700	$24,000	7.58	$14,000	$3,167	$6,334	$9,501	$15,835
Jul-07	$330,700	$125	0.04	$0	$3,307	$6,614	$9,921	$16,535
Aug-07	$330,700	$1,950	0.59	$0	$3,307	$6,614	$9,921	$16,535
Sep-07	$322,650	$27,500	8.52	$17,500	$3,227	$6,453	$9,680	$16,133
Oct-07	$340,150	$15,000	4.41	$5,000	$3,402	$6,803	$10,205	$17,008
Nov-07	$345,150	$21,500	6.23	$11,500	$3,453	$6,903	$10,355	$17,258
Dec-07	$356,650	$17,525	4.91	$7,525	$3,567	$7,133	$10,700	$17,833
Jan-08	$364,175	$25,000	6.86	$15,000	$3,642	$7,284	$10,925	$18,209
Feb-08	$379,175	$39,000	10.29	$29,000	$3,792	$7,584	$11,375	$18,959
Mar-08	$408,175	-$18,000	-4.41	$0	$4,082	$8,164	$12,245	$20,409
Apr-08	$408,175	-$22,000	-5.39	$0	$4,082	$8,164	$12,245	$20,409
May-08	$376,175	$24,750	6.58	$14,750	$3,762	$7,524	$11,285	$18,809
Jun-08	$390,925	$12,000	3.07	$2,000	$3,909	$7,819	$11,728	$19,546
Jul-08	$392,925	$19,500	4.96	$9,5000	$3,929	$7,859	$11,788	$19,646

Table D.1

Bo Yoder's
Profit Compounding Worksheet
www.boyoder.com

What Is Your
Monthly Nut?

Date	Account	Monthly P/L	%Return	Compound $$	1% Risk	2% Risk	3% Risk	5% Risk

Table D.2

EXECUTION GPA WORKSHEET

Finding a valid and sustainable edge is a sometimes difficult and time-consuming task. There is no reason to throw away edge on mistakes, slippage, and other costly trading "overhead." The *Execution GPA Worksheet* is a handy way to track how much money was lost due to these hidden drags on performance.

As a beginner, you may wish to identify separate sheets for mental errors, execution errors, and emotional missteps. Since the majority of my execution problems are due to fast market conditions or "fat finger trades" (buying 18 contracts instead of 15), I just group them all together on one sheet. Ironically enough, the only mental error I catch myself making consistently these days is what I call "directional dyslexia." I will go short by mistake when I think the market is about to go up, long by mistake when I think the market is about to go down. Because of my ritualistic trade checklist, I always catch these errors within seconds, but they still cost me commissions and a tick or two so they end up on my *Execution GPA Worksheet.*

Bo Yoder's
Execution GPA Worksheet
www.boyoder.com

Trade Checklist

Did I get my entire position filled?
Is my stop-loss order correct and live?
Is my position taken in the correct direction?
Is my take profit order correct and live?
Are all my open orders for the correct/same size?
Are any unwanted open orders live?

Date	Time of Day	Type of error	Cost in $$	Instrument	Running Total	Grade Error

Table E.1

INDEX

ABOUT THE AUTHOR

Bo Yoder is a professional trader, author, and consultant to the financial industry on matters of trading edge and risk management. His interest in the business of trading began in the early 1990s when a small investment held over the winter brought in as much income as it did working as a ski instructor. This experience led to a change in direction as Bo left his job to begin trading and investing full time. After a period of intense study and research, he created a suite of unique trading strategies he still uses today to gain an edge in the world's markets.

Best known as the originator of the payout/payback cycle and liquidity pool theory, Bo can be seen as a featured speaker internationally at seminars and industry events. Bo continues to work with individuals and market professionals on optimizing their edge through his live events, Webinars, and DVD series.

When not speaking or working with private clients, Bo enjoys the freedom that remote trading delivers and splits his time between his home in Maine, and just about any location across the globe that offers a reliable Internet connection to the financial markets.